CONTENTS

INTRODUCTION

Thailand's tropical landscape and happy-go-lucky people have won such enormous world acclaim that the 'Land of Smiles' now plays host to more travellers than almost any other destination in Asia. This bountiful kingdom, which is about the same size as France, offers great variety: from rice fields and dense forest to palm-fringed beaches and idyllic islands, as well as ancient cities. To crown it all, the Thai food, which combines subtle flavours, will delight discerning visitors.

Here you can enjoy the sight of saffron-robed monks wandering the streets at dawn and markets piled high with exotic fruits and vegetables. Add to this the many historic sights, the magnificent festivals and the varied countryside and you have a country that for many has no equal.

Not all first-time visitors will appreciate Bangkok, with its traffic jams and its sheer unutterable chaos, but beneath the excesses this city, with no less than 400 temples, does have a heart. In the south, the famous beach resorts of Phuket and Ko Samui are memorable, with their turquoise seas and white sparkling beaches. Up in the north, especially in the hills around Mae Hong Son, there are plenty of other natural attractions.

More than anything though, it is the people and their delightful traditions that continue to make Thailand one of the most popular and rewarding tourist destinations in the Far East.

An elaborately gilded temple guard outside the Wat Phra Kaeo (Temple of the Emerald Buddha), Bangkok.

GEOGRAPHY

Thailand is situated in the very heart of
south-east Asia, bordered to the north by
Burma and Laos, to the east by Cambodia
and to the south by Malaysia. Within its
landmass of 517 000 sq km (199 613 square
miles), it has everything from mountains
and tropical beaches to rain forest and
turquoise seas. Shaped like an elephant's
head, it measures 1 800km (1 118 miles)
from top to bottom, and just 22km (13.6
miles) at the narrowest point along the

trunk-like southern isthmus. Thailand's tropical climate and abundant rivers have also made this one of the most fertile countries in the world. Little surprise, then, that it exports more than 20 million tons of rice a year, as well as numerous varieties of beautiful orchids.

Central Plain

The heart of Thailand is the Central Plain, a rich and fertile area stretching from Bangkok to Phitsanulok, which forms the country's major rice-growing region.

In the northern part of the plains, the rivers Ping, Yom and Nan unite to form the Chao Phraya – 'mother of waters', the lifeline for the vast Mae Nam Basin. Further to the west lies Kanchanaburi, home of the famous bridge over the River Kwai, as well as countless waterfalls, caves and national parks. Within easy reach of Bangkok, other attractions abound, ranging from the floating market at Damnoen Saduak to the salt plains near Samut Sakhon.

Northern Thailand

Compared with the central region, Northern Thailand offers even greater diversity. Although its mountains cannot equal the Alps (Doi Inthanon, the country's highest peak, rises to 2 568m/8 425ft), it does have valleys and forests, populated by numerous ethnic groups who have migrated from China, Burma and Laos. Major rivers, including the Mekong, Nan, Yom, Ping and the Wang, run across this landscape, providing a rich natural backdrop. In north-east Thailand, however, much of the forest has been cut down, and drought and flooding are now frequent in this region.

One of the many rivers flowing through the Mae Hong Son Province, Northern Thailand, with the mountains beyond.

Beaches and Islands

Southern Thailand consists of a strip of land averaging 64km (40 miles) wide and about 1 250km (775 miles) long. Known as the Kra Peninsula, it borders Burma in the north-west and Malaysia to the south. Islands and sparkling white beaches are the hallmarks of the southern region, along with turquoise seas, rubber plantations and mountainous foothills rising as high as 2 000m (6 562ft). You can take your pick from a range of tropical havens as well as international-class resorts offering every form of luxury.

There is a distinct difference between the two coasts. Along the west coast limestone formations predominate, including the fantastical towering rocks at Phangnga and around Krabi, and a coastline with numerous bays, islands, spectacular coastal scenery and outstanding coral reefs. Phuket Island is one of Thailand's top beach resorts on this coast. Along the central ridge of the peninsula are mountains covered with tropical vegetation, while the east coast has fine sandy beaches, backed by these stunning mountains, and a sprinkling of beautiful islands, making the region especially popular with tourists.

The beautiful islands of Ko Phi Phi, Southern Thailand.

HISTORY

Nobody can blame the Thais for being proud of their history. Their country not only gave birth to one of the earliest Bronze Age civilisations, but it is also one of the few countries in south-east Asia never to have been colonised by the West. There are plenty of ancient cities too, from **Sukhothai** to **Ayutthaya**, as well as **Lopburi**, which testify to past glory.

These reliefs, from the temple of Hin Phanom Rung, show the Khmer people's gods.

Early Origins

According to archaeologists, Thailand may have had one of the first **Bronze Age** civilisations. Artefacts recently discovered in the town of Ban Chiang, in the north-east region, have been reliably dated as far back as 6 800 BC. They include not only pottery and weapons, but glass beads, sandstone moulds and the world's oldest known socketed tool. If the estimates are true, they may predate similar finds in Mesopotamia.

From about the 6C onwards, ancient **Siam** was made up of a series of small, powerful fiefdoms, constantly battling with each other. The **Mons**, an ancient Indianised people, the **Khmers** from Cambodia and the northern **Lanna** kingdom (especially during the reign of the great **King Mengrai**) have all played significant parts in its history. The Khmers left behind them the magnificent temples of Prasat Hin Phimai, Prasat Muang Tham and Prasat Hin Phanom Rung, as well as striking reliefs of their 'god kings'. Yet while these early kingdoms profoundly influenced the development of Thailand, it was the rebellion by two local rulers against the Khmers that heralded the beginnings of the first unified state.

Sukhothai

The founding of Sukhothai in 1238
signalled the birth of the Thai nation, and
led to a period of outstanding artistic
output. Inspired by Buddhist ideals, the
people created fine sculptures as well as a
succession of great temples which can be
viewed in Sukhothai and in the nearby cities
of Si Satchanalai and Kamphaeng Phet.

This artistic flowering led to the creation
of the first Thai alphabet under the

enlightened reign of **King Ram Kamhaeng the Great** (c1279-1299). Early inscriptions from this period recall a golden age when benevolence and justice were upheld by the rulers, and when fish and rice could be found in abundance throughout the kingdom. Art and architecture flourished, particularly in the reign of **King Li Thai** (1347-1368).

For more than 100 years, Sukhothai remained the dominant power, stretching from Lampang in the north to Vientiane (Laos), and south towards the Malay Peninsula. Its influence weakened, however, and in 1378 it became a vassal state of **Ayutthaya**, which had built its capital at the confluence of the Chao Phraya, Pa Sak and Lopburi rivers.

This 13C Sukhothai Buddha sits proudly in a ruined temple.

Ayutthaya

The most legendary of all the kingdoms of Siam, Ayutthaya dominated the region for the next 400 years. Much of what we know from this period is from contemporary accounts by European, especially French, visitors who describe a kingdom made up of tree-lined streets with sparkling towers and hundreds of pagodas stretching as far as the eye can see. Architecturally, Ayutthaya had no equal. Directors of the East India Company claim that it had a population of over one million people, as well as hundreds of exquisite temples and more than 48km (30 miles) of roads and waterways.

The kingdom reached its peak in the 17C, especially under **King Narai the Great**. Trade in commodities from spice to teak had

These fine wooden carvings recount tales of the Buddha.

positioned Ayutthaya as a key staging post between China, the East Indies and the West. During these opulent years the Portuguese, the Dutch and the French competed to establish close relations with the kings of Siam. Diplomatic ties were established and Siamese envoys attended the court of Louis XIV of France.

An era of struggle and decline ensued. The Burmese invaded on several occasions with their elephants and their foot soldiers. Finally, this turbulent period came to an end in 1767 when, after a 14-month siege, the city fell. Overnight, Ayutthaya's glorious monuments were burnt and pillaged and its golden statues melted down.

Today, we can still enjoy the remains of Ayutthaya and the impressive temples of Wat Phra Si Sanphet, Wat Ratchaburana and Wat Phra Ram. Statues, reliefs and rare frescoes are displayed in the town's museum and in the National Museum in Bangkok.

The Chakri Dynasty

The end of Ayutthaya was rapidly followed by the rise of two new capitals. **Thonburi** was initially chosen, but in 1782 **King Rama I** decided to move the capital again – this time to **Bangkok**, 'village of plums', on the east bank of the Chao Phraya river.

Historians credit Rama I and his successors as the fathers of the Thai nation. They built roads, railways and schools, and introduced western medicine and the first Thai printing press. They also instituted many reforms in order to modernise the country and develop its economy. Some kings were especially famous. **Rama IV**, known as **King Mongkut**, spent 27 years as a monk before emerging to sire 83 children by

35 wives. Mongkut was also a progressive monarch. He spoke seven foreign languages, including Latin and English, and was an expert in astronomy.

His reforms were taken up by a succession of great kings, none more notable than **Rama V**, **Chulalongkorn** (1868-1910), named the Beloved Great King and the Lord of the White Elephant for his contributions to the modern state.

Modern Thailand

The impact of the Chakri kings was widely felt and can still be seen throughout Thailand. The military has played a no less influential role. Since the end of the absolute monarchy in 1932, the kingdom has been buffeted by 17 coups and attempted coups, and countless changes of government.

For all its political theatricality, however, Thailand remains one of the most stable countries in the region. Its king, its Buddhist religion and its racial harmony have enabled the kingdom to avoid the conflicts suffered by many neighbouring countries. Since 1988, Thailand has also been ruled by a democratic government, although the military continues to play a significant part.

The Monarchy

If the Thais are proud of their history, they are even prouder of their monarchy. **King Bhumibol Adulyadej**, ninth in line of the Chakri dynasty, is not only the head of state and leader of the armed forces but also is viewed as guardian of the people. The King is revered in the cities as well as the provinces, where he has travelled extensively to identify the needs of the rural Thais.

THE PEOPLE AND CULTURE

The Thais are a delightful people who worry as little about tomorrow as they did about yesterday, and who can find reason to laugh at even the most disagreeable incident. The two words that you will most commonly hear are *sanuk*, which means 'fun', and *mai pen rai*, which means 'don't worry'. The Thais have taken both words to an extreme: who cares if there is traffic and noise when the food is good and there is rice whisky in abundance.

Thais are instinctively polite and disarmingly charming, with a smile that has made them famous throughout the world. They are also superstitious, whimsical and marvellously inconsistent. Never have your hair cut on a Wednesday. Never move house on a Saturday. These and other superstitions exact as much influence on the Thai people as Buddhism – their national religion.

Light-heartedness and spontaneity are likeable attributes of the people, but saving face is an important social consideration which outsiders should take into account.

Thailand is known as 'The Land of Smiles' for good reason.

Native Thais
Unlike neighbouring Malaysia, Thailand boasts an exceptional ethnic uniformity.

More than 85 per cent of Thailand's 55 million inhabitants claim to be native Thai. These people came from **Yunnan** in Southern China sometime after the 10C, spreading down into the Central Plain along the banks of the Chao Phraya river.

In the north of Thailand and around Chiang Mai, you will find more than 400 000 **hill-tribes** people who have crossed over the borders from Laos, Burma and China and who eke out an existence through slash-and-burn agriculture – and, more recently, tourism. **Karen** and **Hmong** are the most numerous of the hill-tribes people, followed by the **Lahu** and **Akha**. At the far extreme are the elusive **Yellow Leaf** or **Mrabri** tribe, that number just a few hundred families.

Chiang Mai is renowned for its beautiful women, and its colourful processions.

In the north-east region of Thailand you will also encounter the delightful **Isan** people. These rugged, easy-going people come from the poorest area of the country and in many cases originate from Laos. Indeed, it is calculated that there are more Lao people in north-east Thailand than there are in Laos itself.

There are also some five million **Chinese**, found mainly in the commercial centres. Concentrated near the border with Malaysia are an estimated two million people who practise the **Muslim** religion.

The Arts

Thais have a very developed aesthetic sense. Look in their markets and you will see them cutting fruits and vegetables into objects of extraordinary beauty or creating exquisite wood carvings by hand. In their homes, intricate flower displays are fashioned from banana leaves adorned with jasmine or lotus flowers. Even their traditional teak houses are often veritable works of art. The greatest of all art, however, is reserved for their temples and their reliefs and sculptures of the Buddha achieving *nirvana* and ultimate enlightenment.

Nobody should miss a display of classical dancing, the most highly regarded form of entertainment in Thailand. Typically, the dances are based on stories from the *Ramakien*, the Thai equivalent of the Indian *Ramayana*, and feature brightly coloured masks and intricate movements.

Fine murals, often richly-decorated with gold, are a feature of Bangkok's temples.

Buddhism

Buddhism underpins all aspects of life in Thailand. It is apparent everywhere, from the glittering temples to the finely carved sculptures, and from young novices to saffron-robed monks on their early-morning alms round. Every time Thai Airways International, the national airline, inaugurates a new aeroplane, the chief patriarch, who is the head of the monkhood, will give his blessing. Buddhism is an indispensable reminder both of the transitory nature of life and of the means by which man can transcend it.

According to early inscriptions, Buddhism was brought to Thailand in the 13C by missionaries sent out by the Emperor Ashoka of India. Today in Thailand there are more than 28 000 temples and five million Buddha statues; more than 90 per cent of the population claim to be Buddhist. But Buddhism is no typical religion. Rather it is a philosophy that eschews extremes: never kill, never steal, never commit an act of evil. These are just some of the directives that any

Buddhist must take to heart. Good deeds are seen as a way to secure a better position in the next life, while bad deeds may be punished by being reborn as an inferior being.

In many parts of Thailand, it is still common for a young man to spend several weeks or months as a novice in order to gain merit for himself and his family. During their time in the temple, monks and novices must follow a strict regime. They have to observe a list of 227 rules and must abstain from sex and alcohol, can eat only before midday and must refrain from killing any living thing, even an insect.

Most Thais find little

problem in loosely adhering to the main principles of Buddhism, while at the same time making offerings to countless spirits which inhabit the world. For them, Buddhism provides a moral code and a way to make amends for past acts. It also instils in them a sense of tolerance, of hope and, typically, an unending sense of fun.

Left: Buddhist monks collect their alms at dawn.
Below: Making offerings to the spirits is a part of everyday life.

MUST SEE

There are so many wonderful things to see in Thailand that naming the top ten sights is like having to choose between peaches and pineapples – and inevitably you will have your own favourites. Here, however, is a list of the attractions you should try not to miss.

Grand Palace, Bangkok★★★

A fairytale world of palaces and temples that has no comparison anywhere else in Thailand.

Ko Phi Phi★★

Offering some of the most picturesque seascapes and landscapes in the region, this is a place of stunning beauty, with fine swimming in clear waters.

Phuket★★★

Thailand's best-known international resort, with first-rate beaches and hotels and plenty of attractions in the vicinity.

Sukhothai★★★

A historic site evocative of past glory, in a wonderful setting.

Mae Hong Son★★

Tucked into the hills, with unrivalled opportunities for trekking or exploring the surrounding countryside, while offering the comforts of good hotels.

Doi Mae Salong★★

A small town set in magnificent scenery up near the Burmese border.

Northern Hills★★

The spectacular route from Chiang Mai to Pai is the finest in Thailand, although you

should beware of the countless tight bends and sudden drops.

Damnoen Saduak★

Despite the tourists, this delightful floating market brings back memories of what was once a typical scene in Thailand.

Phimai★★★

Prasat Hin Phimai is the best known Khmer-style temple in the country, with elaborate stone carvings and intricate reliefs.

Traditional Festivals

There are many colourful and dramatic re-enactments of age-old festivals to enjoy, such as Loi Krathong at Sukhothai or Chiang Mai.

The Candle Festival at Ubon Ratchathani is a colourful event.

BANGKOK★★★

With over five million people, one million cars and some of the worst traffic problems in Asia, it is no wonder that many tourists take an immediate dislike to Thailand's capital city. But for those who make the effort, Bangkok, known as the 'City of Angels', can offer some magical experiences. In this metropolis, built by Rama I, you can still glimpse golden temples, palaces and churches, as well as sleepy canals and markets overflowing with orchids and lotus flowers. To avoid unnecessary hassles, take a tour and start out early. Finally, remember that patience is the most valuable commodity in Bangkok – and those who have it will discover a city with a heart and soul unlike anywhere else in Asia.

Phra Borom Maharatchawong★★★
(Grand Palace)

The Grand Palace is the single most impressive site in the whole of Thailand, not only because of its vast scale, but because of the mixture of styles and the sheer number of its glittering spires. Begun in 1782, its architecture spans almost 200 years. The succession of ornate monuments we see today covers 2.5 sq km (1 square mile) and until 1946 housed the royal family.

The **Chakri Maha Prasat** is the centrepiece. Completed in 1882 by King Rama V, this splendid building is designed in the neoclassical style. It is crowned by a traditional Thai roof, with three seven-tiered spires that contain the ashes of the eight Chakri kings.

The **Dusit Maha Prasat★** is famous – and rightly so – for its gilded nine-tiered roof

Wat Phra Kaeo, containing the Emerald Buddha, is the holiest shrine in Thailand.

The spires of the Chakri Maha Prasat hold ashes of royal kings and princes.

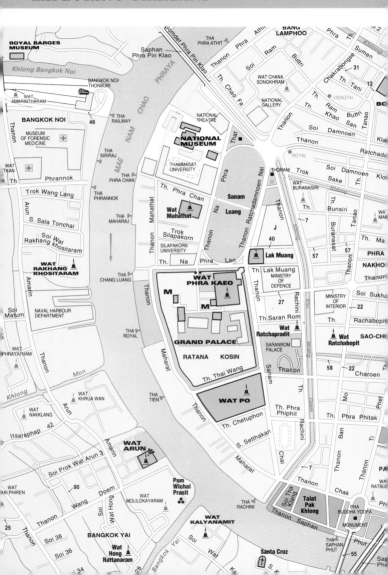

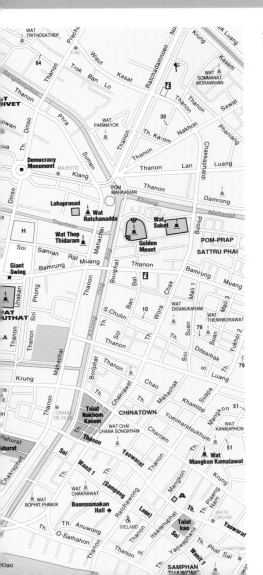

Map of central Bangkok.

supported by mythical birds and dragon-headed serpents. Nearby is the **Aphon Phimok Prasat★★**, a jewel of Thai architecture, with exquisite decorative features, where the monarch changed from his ceremonial robes before stepping into his palanquin.

The *pièce de résistance* is the dazzling **Wat Phra Kaeo★★★** (Temple of the Emerald Buddha), which contains Thai Buddhism's most sacred image, the Emerald Buddha. This diminutive figure, symbolising royalty, sits on an altar protected by a five-tiered umbrella. The interior is equally impressive, with striking murals of the Ramayana, mother-of-pearl windows and Khmer-style bronze lions guarding the entrance. The profusion of decorative elements – gilded mythical animals, multicoloured mosaic and porcelain – is breathtaking.

Palaces and Museums

Although nothing else can really compare with the magnificence of the Grand Palace, Bangkok has plenty of other palaces and royal houses worth a visit. **Vimanmek Palace★★★**, a former residence of King Chulalongkorn, is visually stunning not only because of its sheer size (it is one of the largest teak houses in the world), but also because of its texture and colouring. Inside the building, which is situated diagonally opposite the Dusit Zoo (*see* p.36), there is a treasure-trove of memorabilia, from mounted elephant tusks to betel-nut boxes, and even the first shower believed to have been used in Thailand.

A striking collection of wooden buildings can be seen at **Suan Pakkard Palace★★**, the former home of the late Princess Chumphot

Despite its vast size and elaborate design, the Vimanmek Palace was built in just seven months.

of Nagara Svarga, situated near the Phayathai intersection on Si Ayutthaya Road. An avid gardener, she left magnificent gardens with several rare plants, as well as the exquisite **Lacquer Pavilion★★★**, dating from the early Bangkok period and decorated in distinctive Thai style of gilt on black laqueur.

The **National Museum★★★** on Na Phra That Road is one of Asia's finest museums. Among its splendid buildings are **Phra Thinang Phutthaisawan**, a royal chapel dating from 1782, and **Tamnak Daeng★★**, a former royal residence in red teakwood. Its precious works of art include pottery excavated from **Ban Chiang**, stone and

bronze statues, gold regalia and ceramics, as well as ornate funeral chariots.

Jim Thompson's House★★, on Soi Kasemsan 2, comprises seven fine teak houses built on the banks of a canal which provides a wonderful insight into life in old Bangkok, as well as containing a priceless collection of paintings, porcelain and statues. Its owner, a famous silk merchant known as the 'Silk King', was also rumoured to be a CIA agent. Jim Thompson disappeared in the Cameron Highlands in Malaysia in 1967. Despite repeated searches, no trace of his body was ever found.

The massive reclining Buddha in Wat Po, Bangkok, is covered in gold-leaf.

Temples

When in the vicinity of the Grand Palace, visit **Wat Po★★** on Maharat Road, the oldest and largest temple complex in Bangkok. Originally built in the 16C, this favourite temple of the early Chakri kings houses a gigantic reclining Buddha measuring 46m (150ft) long and 15m (49ft) high. The statue is entirely covered with gold-leaf, and the soles of its feet are inlaid with mother-of-pearl depicting the 108 characteristics of the Buddha.

From nearby **Wat Arun★★** (Temple of Dawn), you can enjoy fine views of the Chao

The temple of Wat Arun is decorated with mosaics created from pieces of porcelain.

Phraya river and the distant Grand Palace. Built during the second half of the 19C, the highlight of this temple is the central pagoda, decorated with millions of pieces of porcelain arranged in the shape of flowers.

There are many interesting temples, such as **Wat Benchamabopit**★★ (Marble Temple) on Si Ayutthaya Road, to the north of the Grand Palace, which boasts elaborately adorned gables and impressive marble porches. Here you can watch monks collecting alms at dawn. In **Wat Traimit**, near the intersection of Yaowarat and Charoen Krung roads, you will find the biggest gold **Buddha image**★★ in Thailand, weighing in at 5.5 tons (5 tonnes). It was discovered to be

made of gold by chance when workmen dropped the stucco-covered statue from a crane. **Wat Saket** on Chakkaphatdi Phong Road, one of the earliest temples in Bangkok, and **Wat Thong Nophakhun** in Thonburi, feature delightful mural paintings.

Other Attractions

A boat trip on the **Chao Phraya river** is a must, especially if you are in Bangkok during the dry season. From the relative calm of the water you can admire the chaotic vistas around you, and get a sense of how life was in the days when, criss-crossed by networks of canals, the city was known as the 'Venice of the East'. Long-tail boats depart from the **Tha Chang Pier**, outside the Grand Palace, and from the major river hotels for brief tours of **Wat Arun★★**, the **Royal Barge Museum★** and **Khlong Noi** and **Khlong Yai**. River trips generally take an hour (remember to agree on a price beforehand).

At the busy **Weekend Market**, near the southern end of Chatuchak Park, you can buy anything from ancient pots to live snakes and aphrodisiacs. Among this mind-boggling display of goods you may even find Dickensian novels and old copies of *Time Magazine*. **Pak Khlong Market**, near the Tha Rachini Pier on the Chao Phraya river, is where locals come to buy their fresh produce, ranging from orchid flowers and pigs' trotters to the highly-prized but pungent-smelling fruit known as the *durian*. **Klongtoey Market**, off Rama IV Road, provides plenty of local colour, as well as cheap T-shirts, radios and household items.

Cobras and spotted vipers can be seen at

The Wat Arun at sunset is a magical sight, seen from across the Chao Phraya river.

Temples

Temples, or *wats*, are distinctive features of Thailand. Some contain glittering golden spires, others monumental statues of the Buddha or of famous local monks. In Bangkok alone, there are more than 400 temples, with another 28 000 throughout the rest of the kingdom.

Look inside any one of these houses of worship and you will find people meditating, lighting joss sticks or making offerings to the Buddha in the hope of accumulating merit for the next life. Listen to the villagers and you will hear them asking advice from the monks on subjects ranging from what name to call a newly-born child, to problems involving a family member. Visit on the occasion of a religious festival and you will come across large numbers of followers listening to Buddhist scriptures or processing three times around the temple compound, carrying lighted candles.

Many of Thailand's greatest works of art are also to be found inside the temples, such as fine statues of the

Buddha, sculptures of the great *naga* serpent or striking mural paintings. As you grow more accustomed to religious art, you will notice the subtle changes in the depiction of the Buddha, from the rigid symmetry of the pre-Khmer period (5C-11C) to the serene oval faces of the Sukhothai period (13C-15C). You may also notice how the temples themselves have become increasingly stylised.

Take some time to familiarise yourself with the most common architectural terms used to describe a Thai temple. Below is a simple list.

ubosot, bot: ordination hall where important religious rites are held

chedi: bell-like structure or pagoda, often containing holy relics

prang: rounded tower, often containing holy relics

prasat: sanctuary constructed by the Khmers

stupa: tower or pagoda, often a burial site

vihara: hall for daily worship

wat: temple or monastery.

Left: The golden Buddha at Phra Sri Rattana Mahathat, Phitsanulok. Below: Fine murals adorn many temples.

the Snake Farm or **Pasteur Institute** on Rama IV Road. These and other venomous reptiles are milked daily for their serum, which acts as an antidote for snake bites. At the **Dusit Zoo** on Rama V Road you will find more snakes, as well as over 300 mammals, including elephants and rhinoceros. Avoid weekends though, when the place is crowded with locals. **Chinatown** is famous for its bustling atmosphere and fascinating sights.

To escape the hustle and bustle of Bangkok, visit **Lumphini Park** on the corner of Rama IV and Silom Road. Here in the centre of town you will find a haven of calm, with grassy lawns, shady walkways and a lake with paddle-boats which can be hired by the hour.

Patpong Road is not only known for its bars and licentious entertainment but also for its night market (*see* p.104).

The Wat Benchamabopit is known as the Marble Temple because of its Carrara marble walls.

EXCURSIONS FROM BANGKOK

Explore the area within a three-hour radius of Bangkok and you will discover a host of attractions, ranging from ancient cities to historic bridges, and the famous floating market of Damnoen Saduak. Tours can be arranged for the day, although longer trips may prove more enjoyable.

Muang Boran** (Ancient City)

The magnificent outdoor museum at the Ancient City, near Samut Prakan, is designed in the geographical outline of Thailand. Authentic recreations of all the great temples and the most beautiful and famous monuments are set in their exact location. There are also traditional wooden houses, palaces and a floating market.

As a change from Thailand's cultural masterpieces, take a short drive to the

Hungry mouths awaiting their next meal at the Crocodile Farm, Samut Prakan.

nearby **Crocodile Farm**, at Samut Prakan. Here you can watch demonstrations of crocodile wrestling and observe up to 30 000 of the scaly creatures sunning themselves, eating and sleeping. The farm also has a

37

licence to export crocodile leather. Crocodile handbags and belts are on sale outside, but so far there are no croc-burgers!

Damnoen Saduak*

Barely two hours' drive to the south-west of Bangkok, the floating market of Damnoen Saduak is a colourful spectacle. On the narrow *khlongs* (canals) in **Ratchaburi** Province, vendors in large-brimmed hats paddle merrily around in wooden boats laden with exotic fruits, vegetables and cooked delicacies – much as they have done

The chaotic jumble of boat stalls jostling for position at the floating market of Damnoen Saduak.

for centuries. You can rent a boat and join the throng, or simply take photos from the overhead bridges. To avoid the coach tours, get there early. Late-comers get the market without the real vendors, but with snake charmers and postcard sellers in abundance.

Kanchanaburi★★

Despite its magical setting at the confluence of the Khwae Yai and the Khwae Noi, this little town 130km (80 miles) to the west of Bangkok possesses a less than magical history. It was here during the Second World

The famous 'Bridge over the River Kwai' is a sombre memorial to those who lost their lives in its construction.

War that thousands of prisoners of war died building the notorious '**Bridge over the River Kwai**', which was intended to connect Japanese-occupied Singapore with Rangoon in Burma. They are remembered in the moving **War Cemetery** on Saeng Chuto Road containing the graves of 6 982 servicemen, and at the **Chung Kai Cemetery** on the banks of the Kwai River, which contains a further 1 750 gravestones. At the **JEATH War Museum**, on Paak Phraek Road, there is a replica of a prisoner-of-war hut, with a collection of photographs and haunting paintings.

Despite its sombre undertones, modern Kanchanaburi has an attractive side. Long-boats can be hired from under the bridge for a river tour, stopping at the cave of **Wat Thum Khao Phun** as well as the JEATH War Museum. Also not to be missed is the fantastic **train ride**★★ along sheer gorges to **Nam Tok**, a small village which marks the end of the line. There are several beauty spots outside the town, including the **Erawan National Park**★★, which lies 70km (43 miles) to the north, and the **Sai Yok National Park**★★, some 100km (62 miles) to the west.

Khao Yai★★★

Thailand's oldest national park, situated 200km (124 miles) to the north-east of Bangkok, is famous for its luxuriant trees, waterfalls, walking trails and hills. Elephants, wild pigs or fallow deer may be spotted, together with rare birds such as the orange-breasted and red-headed trogons and moustached barbets, as well as countless hornbills. Within the 2 169 sq km (837 square miles) park, are the delightful waterfalls of **Nam Tok Heo Suwat**★★ and **Nam Tok Pha Kluai Mai**, as well as impressive views from the mountain tops at **Khao Laem** (1 328m/4 357ft) or **Khao Khieo** (1 350m/4 429ft). Avoid weekends when the park is crowded and the rainy season when armies of leeches are on the loose.

Ko Samet★

Magnificent beaches, crystal-clear waters and tropical vegetation make this idyllic island the perfect 'getaway'. Situated a three-hour drive away from Bangkok and a 30-minute boat ride from the small fishing village at **Ban Phe**, its beauty was first

The island of Ko Samet offers wonderful beaches and azure seas, in a tropical setting.

celebrated by the famous 19C poet Sunthorn Phu who lived here for many years. The island offers simple accommodation, and its lovely bays and relaxed atmosphere give the place a special charm.

Hat Sai Kaew★★ is the main stretch of white sandy beach, with bungalows dotted along its full length. Further south is the smarter **Ao Wong Duan**, in a long, crescent-shaped bay. A sprinkling of other beaches and rocky coves are to be found at **Ao Thian** and **Ao Wai**, situated close to the southern tip of the island.

The island is very busy at weekends, so try to visit mid-week. There are facilities for snorkelling and windsurfing, and it is the place to enjoy fine seafood.

Nakhon Pathom★

This little town 56km (34 miles) west of Bangkok claims to be the place where Buddhism was first introduced in the 3C by Indian missionaries to Thailand. To celebrate, its inhabitants built a *chedi* (pagoda) so vast that it could be seen from far afield. The latest structure, the **Phra Pathom Chedi★★**, which was begun in 1853 by King Mongkut, is 120m (393ft) high. It is most popular in November when the **Phra That Phanom** homage-paying fair is held.

Pattaya★★

It was not so long ago that this town, 150km (93 miles) to the south-east of Bangkok, was regarded as Thailand's premier international beach resort. Over-building, prostitution and pollution have tarnished its image but a determined effort is being made to remedy the situation. Along the beach promenade, bars are more numerous than bathers and the high standards of the hotels and restaurants, plus the sheer array of entertainment centres, make it worth a visit.

The beach at Pattaya is backed by hotels and bars, but it remains relatively uncrowded.

Several nearby islands, **Ko Larn**, **Ko Sak** and **Ko Khrok**, can be reached on converted fishing trawlers and offer good opportunities for snorkelling and diving. Three kilometres (2 miles) further south, **Hat Jomtien★** offers better beaches for swimming, as well as a full range of watersports and facilities for parasailing, windsurfing and deep-sea fishing.

Family activities in the vicinity include the popular **Mini Siam** with models of Thailand's monuments, and the **Million-Year Stone Park**, which has amazing rock formations. Children may prefer **Pattaya Park**, featuring giant waterslides, restaurants

and a swimming pool.

Around 15km (9 miles) to the south-east of town is **Suan Nong Nooch**, which boasts magnificent orchid gardens, a lotus village, a mini-zoo and a swimming pool. Various shows bring to life local pastimes, ranging from traditional dance and cockfighting to Thai boxing and elephant riding.

Pattaya's nightlife has provided the town with a different reputation. Bars, clubs, discos and transvestite shows are the rule rather than the exception and, despite valiant efforts to clean up its image, almost anything goes.

Phimai

The Khmer temple, **Prasat Hin Phimai★★★**, situated in the small town of Phimai, a three-hour drive to the north-east of Bangkok, cannot fail to impress. Built some time during the 12C, it is ranked as one of the best examples of classic Khmer architecture in the entire region.

The symmetrical design is typical of the period. The elegant courtyards and fine sandstone carvings recall the Khmer cosmos and the legendary Mount Meru, realm of the Gods. There are intricate engravings of flowers, elephants and monkeys as well as stone statues of lions that frame the entrance. In the inner courtyard, there is a truly magnificent statue of the Buddha.

The Khmer temple of Prasat Hin Phimai is noted for its fine stone carvings.

Renovation of Prasat Hin Phimai was completed in the 1970s by the Thai Fine Arts Department.

Temple enthusiasts who do not mind travelling further afield can visit **Prasat Hin Phanom Rung★★★**, 100km (62 miles) to the south-east of Khorat, which is claimed by some archaeologists to be even finer than Phimai. The temple is approached by a stone avenue constructed by Jayavarman VII. The magnificent carved lintels adorning the doorways are famous. Even more striking are the engravings of **Kala**, the God of Time and Death. A further 7km (4 miles) to the east is **Prasat Muang Tham★★**, another splendid temple with some fine carvings based on Brahman mythology.

The ruins of Prasat Muang Tham are not so well-preserved, but the temple is a very evocative site.

CENTRAL REGION

This region along the Chao Phraya Valley is one of the most prolific rice-growing areas in the world, and is famous for the ancient towns of Ayutthaya, Lopburi and Sukhothai. It can be explored from Bangkok or used as a stepping-stone to the northern region.

Ayutthaya★★★
If you fancy a day out from Bangkok with some culture thrown in, you could take a leisurely river cruise to **Ayutthaya**, the ancient capital of Siam, which is less than a

This river boat in Ayutthaya offers a different way to see the sights.

three-hour trip away from Bangkok on the Chao Phraya river. This great kingdom ruled for more than 400 years before it was captured and pillaged by the Burmese in 1767.

Any tour should take in the impressive **Wat Phra Si Sanphet★★**, whose three restored *chedis* (pagodas) still loom over the surrounding countryside. Built in the 14C,

46

this temple once contained a 16m (52ft) Buddha image covered in gold. In the nearby **Wihan Phra Mongkol Bophit** there is a monumental seated bronze Buddha dating back to the 15C.

Even better known is **Wat Ratchaburana★★** which marks the site where two princes killed one another in a duel on elephant-back. It was built in 1434 and has giant gateways, soaring *prangs* (towers) with fine stucco decoration and rare mural paintings in the crypt. Other temples worth visiting are the imposing **Wat Phra Mahathat**, which is one of the oldest ruins, and **Wat Chai**

The three pagodas of Wat Phra Si Sanphet form a striking landmark.

This Buddha is seated in front of the Khmer-style tower of Wat Ratchaburana.

The summer palace at Bang Pa-In combines Siamese, Greek, Italian and Chinese styles of architecture.

Wattanaram★★, believed to symbolise the abode of heavenly gods.

Ayutthaya also boasts two fine museums. The **Chao Sam Phraya National Museum★★** displays a collection of stone and bronze Buddha images dating as far back as the 13C, remarkable door panels with religious and floral carvings, and glittering **treasure★★★**. The **Chandra Kasem Palace** presents art objects from Ayutthaya's greatest temples.

A 20-minute drive to the south of Ayutthaya is another marvel, the palace at **Bang Pa-In★★**. It was built by King Prasat Thong in the 17C and subsequently used as a summer residence by a succession of kings. There are a number of striking buildings from the **Warophat Phiman** (Excellent and Shining Abode), to the **Ho Withun Thasana**

(Sage's Lookout) and **Wehat Chamrun★★**, a magnificent Chinese pavilion. The most impressive of all is the **Aisawan Tippaya Asna★★** (Divine Seat of Personal Freedom), situated in the middle of the lake. Scattered around the leafy gardens are a number of statues as well as a monument to King Chulalongkorn's favourite wife and her daughters, who drowned tragically in front of a crowd of onlookers who were barred from coming to their rescue by palace rules.

Lopburi★★
This historic town, 154km (96 miles) north of Bangkok, boasts a number of Khmer ruins, which date back to between the 11C and 13C when this was an important outpost of their empire. Several imposing temples are clustered around the railway line, including the 13C **Wat Phra Sam Yot★★** and the 12C **Wat Phra Si Ratana Mahathat★★**. Other pieces of Khmer art, including a collection of Lopburi-style Buddhas, are to be found in the **National Museum★** at **Phra Narai Ratcha Niwet★★**. The palace was built

The monkeys at San Phra Kan, Lopburi, can be very friendly.

in the 17C by European architects for King Narai who had established a second capital at Lopburi and lived there until his death. Envoys from the court of Louis XIV of France were dazzled by the splendour of the Siamese court. In the newer section of the building you can see giant shadow-puppets as well as much memorabilia from the reign of King Rama IV. The **San Phra Kan** (Kala Shrine) is famous for its resident monkeys.

Sukhothai★★★

The **Historical Park** at Sukhothai, which lies 50km (31 miles) west of Phitsanulok, marks a glorious era in Thailand's history. This great kingdom – which lasted for little more than 100 years – saw the flourishing of some of the greatest art in Siam and ushered in the celebrated Buddha image with its finely balanced composition, its delicate oval face and eyes that radiate calm.

This magnificent Buddha statue, at Sukhothai Historical Park, displays the typical facial characteristics of Buddha images of the period.

For sheer elegance and magic, **Wat Phra Si Mahathat★★★**, Temple of the Great Relic, cannot be excelled. It was built in the 13C and is surrounded by lotus-filled ponds and fine Buddha images silhouetted against some 200 *chedis* (pagodas). Nearby are two other magnificent edifices: **Wat Sa Sri★** (Temple of the Splendid Pond) and **Wat Si Sawai★★** with its three majestic *prangs* (spires), built in the 12C. There are numerous other temples outside the Historical Park, such as **Wat Si Chum★**, with a vast seated Buddha whose fingers are each as big as a man, and **Wat Saphan Hin★**, a

The chedis (pagodas) of Wat Phra Si Mahathat are testimony to the former greatness of Sukhothai.

perfect spot from which to watch the sunset. **Wat Chang Lom** is famous for its elephant buttresses.

Near the entrance to the park, you will find the **Ram Kamhaeng National Museum★★** which houses a superb collection of sculptures, including the celebrated statue of the walking Buddha in the round,

The famous elephant buttresses of Wat Chang Lom, Sukhothai.

and inscriptions unearthed in Sukhothai and the surrounding provinces. If you visit in early November, you will see Sukhothai at its finest when the people celebrate the three-day ceremony of **Loi Krathong**.

For other fine temples, continue 55km (35 miles) north to the town of **Si Satchanalai★★**, the sister city of Sukhothai until the 15C when it was abandoned. The most famous temple there is **Wat Chang Lom★★**, known as the elephant shrine because of its remarkable stucco carvings. Nearby are **Wat Khao Phanom Phloeng★★**, set on the hillside, and the 15C Sinhalese-style **Wat Nang Phaya**.

A reclining Buddha, draped with saffron cloths, Sukhothai.

Kamphaeng Phet★★ is the third of the ancient cities, situated 100km (62 miles) to the south of Sukhothai. It has a historical park with several temple complexes and a splendid reclining Buddha near **Wat Phra Kaeo★★**.

The busy city of **Phitsanulok★** to the east of Sukhothai has only one real claim to fame – it is home to **Wat Phra Sri Rattana Mahathat★★**, which contains the **Phra Phuttha Chinarat★★★**, one of the kingdom's most revered images, covered in thin layers of gold. There are excellent floating restaurants moored along the river, offering a welcome break from sightseeing.

You may be fortunate enough to witness one of the many religious ceremonies, such as this one in the Sukhothai Province.

Rice Farming

Everywhere in the villages and countryside of Thailand rice farmers can be seen hard at work, often up to their knees in the muddy fields or straining to attach a water buffalo to a rickety wooden cart. They form the majority of the Thai people and over the centuries have become the backbone of the Thai nation.

The cycle governs life in the countryside. The rice is planted by hand and the paddies flooded by a series of irrigation channels. Within weeks, a multitude of fragile green shoots has sprouted and the muddy fields are transformed into a vast green lake stretching as far as the eye can see. Soon the land is a sea of gold, broken here and there by the glint of a Buddhist temple. Whole families then descend into the fields along with herds of water buffalo and, working from dawn to dusk, harvest the rice using simple wooden scythes. Finally, the rice fields are burnt off, thereby completing the cycle.

Rice-growing is vital to the economy of Thailand. More than 80 per cent of the population eat rice at least once a day, making this a staple food. In addition, every year Thailand exports 20 million tons of rice to foreign markets.

Although tractors are beginning to replace some of the traditional rice harvesters, it will be many more years before the rice workers are relegated to the past.

These Karen people are working in the rice fields near Mae Sot, in western Thailand.

NORTHERN THAILAND

The area to the north of Bangkok offers a wide range of attractions, from hill-trekking to elephant-riding, and from orchids to northern-style temples.

Chiang Mai★★★

Chiang Mai may seem to be more of a sprawling metropolis than the mountain paradise it has sometimes been described as, but Thailand's second city, which lies 720km (447 miles) north of Bangkok, does have plenty of cultural and historical attractions – along with a cooler climate.

It was founded by King Mengrai during the 13C, and its rich legacy of temples owes much to its former role as capital of the kingdom of **Lanna**. Rebuilt sections of the walls that once surrounded the city on all sides can still be seen. The original walls were constructed by some 90 000 men and a moat was dug to protect the hundreds of temples within.

As you explore the streets of this town, take time to appreciate these great buildings, many of which date back several hundred years. **Wat Chiang Man★** is reputedly the oldest *wat* in the city. It was built by King Mengrai himself and contains the famous **Phra Buddha Setang Khamanai**, a tiny crystal image believed to have the power to bring rain.

Wat Phra Sing Luang★★★ is the largest and most important temple. Built in 1345 by King Pha Yu, it features a graceful library as well as superb examples of wood carving and stucco work. The exquisite **Wihan Lai Khan★★★** enshrines the figure known as **Phra Sing Buddha★**, an early Lanna bronze statue

Fierce dragon-headed serpents (nagas) flank the entrance to the Wat Chedi Luang.

taken from Chiang Rai. No less impressive is **Wat Chedi Luang★**, with an enormous ruined **chedi★** (pagoda) which was damaged by an earthquake over 400 years ago. Legend has it that so long as the nearby gum tree continues to grow, Chiang Mai will be safe.

Outside the city walls are a number of temples that blend Burmese and Lanna styles of architecture, including **Wat Buppharam**, **Wat San Faeng** and **Wat Mahawam**.

Further west is **Wat Suan Dok★★**, known as the Flower Garden Temple, which was built in 1383 and has a fine *chedi*. This is the spot to enjoy spectacular views at sunset.

The **National Museum★** has sculptures

The Wat Buppharam houses a black Buddha made from a single piece of teak.

dating back to the Chiang Mai, Dvaravati, Lopburi and Sukhothai periods, as well as a serene Buddha's head, believed to be part of one of the largest bronzes ever cast in Thailand. Off Wualai Road, there is the impressive **Banyen Folk Art Museum**, a charming old northern-style house with wooden carvings and antiques for sale.

Chiang Mai Zoo is another attraction, with the largest selection of animals in Thailand and access to the **Chiang Mai Arboretum**. Nearby, on the University Campus, is the **Hill Tribe Research Centre** which features a small hill-tribes museum, with all the latest information on the Hmong, the Lisu, the Karen, the Lahu, the Akha and the Yao hill-tribes (*see* pp.66-67).

These magnificent wooden carvings can be seen in the Banyen Folk Art Museum.

EXPLORING THAILAND

A must for any visitor to Chiang Mai is the village of **Bo Sang**, which lies 9km (6 miles) to the east and is famous for its colourful umbrellas. Made in all shapes and sizes, they make perfect presents for friends back home. Along **San Kamphaeng Road**, you will also find handicraft centres selling not only silks and woven cotton, but wood carvings, silver bracelets, ceramics and lacquerware.

There are plenty of other northern artefacts, as well as cheap shirts, triangular cushions, wooden carvings and antiques, at the **Night Market** on Chang Klan Road which is, without doubt, the best night market in the whole of Thailand.

You can watch these beautiful hand-painted umbrellas being made at Bo Sang, near Chiang Mai.

Finally, when in Chiang Mai, check to see whether any religious festivals are being held – the town is famous in Thailand for its boisterous celebrations. Two which should not be missed are **Songkran**, held in mid-April, and **Loi Krathong**, held in late October or early November.

Excursions

Chiang Mai provides the perfect base for exploring the countryside around the north. Travel agents organise everything, from trekking amongst the hill-tribes to touring the nearby orchid farms, elephant camps and national parks.

The colourful Songkran religious festival involves an extended rain-dance, where no-one escapes dry.

Wat Phra That Doi Suthep★★★, situated at the summit of a mountain, 16km (10 miles) to the west of town, is steeped in legend. According to local tradition, the temple was built in 1383 in order to bring an end to a drought that had almost brought the city to its knees. You can admire the sanctuaries, with their gilded *stupas* (pagodas), while enjoying splendid views of the city. About 4km (3 miles) up the road is **Phuping Palace**, which serves as the royal family's northern residence. Another 3km (2 miles) further on is the Hmong tribal village of **Doi Pui**, with stalls selling local arts and crafts.

The popular elephant camp at **Mae Taem**, an hour's drive to the north of Chiang Mai, cannot fail to impress. Shows held twice daily recall the days when elephants were still an integral part of life in the region. After the shows, you can take elephant rides into the nearby forest or short trips on a river raft.

The allure of the **Mae Sa Valley★★** is of a different nature. This area, 15km (9 miles) to the north-west of Chiang Mai, boasts not only a picturesque setting, but attractions ranging from the **Mae Sa Waterfall** to orchid farms and butterfly farms, as well as alpine-style bungalows on the hillside.

Doi Inthanon★★, 50 miles (80km) to the south-west of Chiang Mai, is Thailand's tallest mountain. Rising up to a height of 2 568m (8 425ft), it is surrounded by almost 499 sq km (193 square miles) of national park and moist evergreen forest. Ornithologists claim that the park has some of the most varied bird life in the kingdom. Ashy-throated warblers and yellow-bellied flowerpeckers are just two of the many birds that can be seen, especially in the cooler

Elephant rides through the forest make a memorable end to a visit to the Mae Taem elephant camp.

months between November and February. There are pleasant walks to be enjoyed here – the **Mae Ya Waterfall★** is especially impressive after the monsoon rains.

A pleasant day's trip can be made to **Lamphun★★**, the former capital of the Mon Kingdom of Haripunchai, which lies a 30-minute drive to the south of Chiang Mai. Major temples include the 11C **Wat Phra That Haripunchai★★**, renowned for its giant nine-tiered umbrellas made of gold, and **Wat Chamatewee★**, with its two ancient *chedis* (pagodas) decorated with stucco figures of the Buddha dating back to 1218.

Northern Hill-tribes

There are few people more mysterious than the northern hill-tribes, or *chao doi*, who live in primitive villages. In their elegant costumes with their fine jewellery, they seem enigmatic and other-worldly, the very extreme of the native Thais who inhabit the surrounding areas.

These people number more than 400 000 and inhabit large parts of Thailand around Chiang Rai, Mae Hong Son and Nan provinces.

The first tribes migrated little more than a century ago from southern China, Burma and Tibet, bringing with them their own costumes and sets of

beliefs. They survived largely on slash-and-burn agriculture, growing opium and corn, moving each year in search of more fertile land.

In Thailand today, the experts classify these people into six different groups. The most numerous are the Karen, who are largely concentrated along the western border with Burma. The second most populous are the Hmong, or Meo, who originated in southern China and are characterised by their delicately embroidered costumes and silver necklaces. Other tribes people are the Lisu, the Lahu, the Akha and the striking Yao, or Mien.

These people have, however, been heavily influenced by tourism and by government policies aimed at reducing opium cultivation. Once proud and independent, many today are poor and almost wholly cut off from their traditions, posing for trekkers or selling postcards. Only in a handful of villages do the ancient traditions of these hill-tribes still flourish.

Left: A Lisu girl drying herbs.

Centre: An Akha girl, from the Chiang Rai Province.

Right: Mother and baby from the 'padong' or long-necked tribe, Mae Hong Son Province.

Chiang Rai★★

According to legend, this town, 185km (114 miles) north of Chiang Mai, was founded on the banks of the **Kok river** because one of King Mengrai's favourite white elephants strayed to the spot. For several hundred years it was an important trading centre, but fell to the Burmese in the 16C. Nowadays it is a useful springboard for trips to the scenic **Golden Triangle★★** – the infamous opium-growing region where the borders of Thailand, Burma and Laos meet – as well as the towns of **Mae Sai**, **Chiang Saen★★**, **Chiang Kong** and **Doi Mae Salong★★**.

The most famous temple in Chiang Rai is **Wat Phra Kaeo**. It once housed the revered **Emerald Buddha** and boasts some remarkable carvings. Other memorable

The thousand-year-old temple of Doi Tung is set high on the wooded Doi Tung hill, with far-reaching views.

sights include the seven-spired **Wat Jet Yot** and **Wat Phra That Doi Chom Thong**, which offers fine views of the Kok river.

Mae Sai, 70km (43 miles) to the north, offers plenty of excitement. From this lively little border town you can cross over into the Burmese town of **Tachilek** for the day, so long as you bring a passport and do not stray any further afield. Mae Sai offers fine shopping: Burmese puppets, hill-tribe silver and lacquerware as well as the famous Burmese-style tapestries known as *kalaga*. The hillside temple of **Doi Tung★★** is also worth visiting. It lies an hour's drive west, set amid magnificent countryside where hill-tribes, as part of various royal projects, have been weaned off opium and encouraged to grow cabbages and strawberries instead.

Chiang Rai, known as the gateway to the Golden Triangle, has some of the most spectacular scenery in the north.

Elsewhere, the trafficking of drugs has made this region known around the world. At **Sop Ruak★★**, which lies 40km (25 miles) north of Chiang Rai, tourists by the dozen have their photograph taken at the official spot marking the Golden Triangle and take boat trips on the **Mekong river**.

The nearby town of **Chiang Saen★★** is steeped in history. It was one of the earliest principalities in the north and is renowned for its collection of ruined temples. The oldest is **Wat Pa Sak★**, built in 1295 under King Saen Phu and boasting an impressive collection of stucco and terracotta decorations. Other temples worth visiting are **Wat Phra Buat** and the 10C **Wat Phra That Chom Kitti★**, reputed to house a part of the Buddha's forehead. Arrive just before sunset for fine views over the Mekong river to Laos.

Doi Mae Salong★★, sometimes known as **Santi Khiri**, is a perfect retreat from the plains. This little village, a 90-minute drive to the north-west of Chiang Rai, has a market famous for its tea, ginger wine and aphrodisiacs. In addition, there are some spectacular views from the village of the surrounding valleys. The people here are not Thai, but rather the remnants of the Nationalist Kuomintang Army who fled China with Chiang Khai Shek after the 1949 revolution, setting up first in Burma and more recently in Doi Mae Salong.

Besides being a centre for trips to neighbouring towns and villages, Chiang Rai is popular for **trekking**. Agencies will arrange trips to the hill-tribe villages, ranging from one day to five days and from energetic trekking to comfortable coach tours.

Crossing the Yom river, near Lampang.

Lampang★★

A city 100km (62 miles) south of Chiang Mai, Lampang has many fine temples clustered around the banks of the **Yom river**. Notable are the harmonious **Wat Sri Rong Muang**, **Wat Phra Fang** and **Wat Si Chum**, which contain examples of Burmese-style carvings. **Wat Phra Kaeo Don Tao★★** is especially impressive, with its ceilings of sculptured wood and mother-of-pearl decoration. The temple is believed to enshrine a hair of the Buddha. **Wat Phra That Lampang Luang★★★**, founded in the 5C, is situated 18km (11 miles) south of the town. It contains splendid examples of Lanna architecture, with admirable stuccowork and intricate woodwork.

Mae Hong Son★★

This city is a must for lovers of fine countryside. Just a 40-minute flight from Chiang Mai, Mae Hong Son offers fantastic mountain scenery along with good opportunities for trekking, river-rafting or simply enjoying the mountain air.

Thanks to its isolation, visitors can still feel a world away from almost anywhere else in Thailand. Indeed, it was only in 1965 that the first metalled road was built from Chiang Mai and although tourism has grown in leaps and bounds, this town, known as 'city of a million mists', continues to hold its secrets.

The picturesque Chong Kham Lake provides an attractive setting for this temple.

On the banks of picturesque **Chong Kham Lake** are two of the town's best-known Burmese-style temples, **Wat Chong Kham** and **Wat Chong Klang**. They contain a fine collection of carved wooden figures from Burma. The view of the **market place** at dawn is well worth the visit, with locals and the occasional hill-tribes people intermingling. Afterwards you can visit **Wat Hua Wiang** with its wooden tiered roofs typical of the Burmese style – or climb up to the 19C **Wat Phra That Doi Kong Mu★** with its spectacular panorama of the surrounding hills and valley.

Some of the most rewarding sites are to be found outside the town. Most travel agencies arrange trips to the tribal village of **Mae-O**, which lies 22km (14 miles) to the north near the Burmese border. En route you can stop at the pleasant **Pha Sua Waterfall**. There are also trips to **Baan Mai**, home of the **Padong**, or long-necked people (*see* p.67).

The town of **Pai**, 103km (64 miles) from
Mae Hong Son, is in a wonderful location,
set against hills and the misty Pai river. As
the narrow road snakes its way through the
mountainside, magnificent views of the
valley below unfold. From Pai there are
walks up into the hills or you can simply
relax in bungalows along the river.

Trips can be made to the cave of **Tham
Lot★★**, 45km (28 miles) to the west, near the
town of **Soppong**. Here, at dusk, millions of
swallows and bats are seen in flight in an
unbelievable spectacle. Trekking in this
picturesque region is available from travel
agents in Pai.

*Agriculture is
important in the
fertile valleys of the
Mae Hong Son
Province.*

Nan★★

Locals have long known this province to the
east of Chiang Mai to be one of the least
spoiled in Thailand. There are several
temples in the town dating back to the 14C,
when it was a semi-autonomous principality.
Wat Phumin★★, with its fine murals, and **Wat
Phra That Chae Haeng**, with its naga
staircase and Laotian-influenced *chedi*
(pagoda), are worth viewing. Even more
rewarding are trips beyond the town, with
opportunities for walking and trekking.

*Nan is famous for
its lovely
countryside and its
temples.*

SOUTHERN THAILAND

Thailand's southern coastline is so well
known that beach resorts such as Phuket
and Ko Samui have become international
names. There are plenty of other beaches
and palm-fringed islands too, as well as
inland rubber plantations and limestone
cliffs beyond compare.

*Beached fishing
boats at Hua Hin.*

Hat Yai

You can't go much further south than Hat Yai without crossing over into neighbouring Malaysia. This big, brassy town, 930km (577 miles) south of Bangkok, has a lively market for smuggled goods as well as a legendary collection of massage parlours. A bull-fight is held on the first Saturday of every month.

If these attractions are not to your taste, however, visit nearby **Songkhla★**, a delightful little fishing port 25km (15 miles) to the north-east, which offers plenty of simpler pleasures such as visiting **Songkhla Museum★**, **Wat Machimawat★★** and the **Folklore Museum★**, or hiring a boat out to **Ko Maeo and Ko Nu** (Cat and Mouse Islands).

North of Songkhla, there are countless species of waterfowl at the **Khu Khut Bird Park**, one of Thailand's best-known waterfowl sanctuaries. As well as cormorants, storks, kingfishers and sandpipers, keep your eyes open for the rare pond herons and fishing eagles, which are best seen during the cooler months of November and December.

Hua Hin★★

This beach town, four hours south of Bangkok, was put on the map by Prince Chakrabongse in 1910 when he discovered it while on a hunting trip. Subsequent kings resided in a summer palace here, and there are reminders of the gentrified past at the **Sofitel Central Hua Hin Hotel**, formerly the Old Railway Hotel. The resort has a fine white sandy beach. Golf can be played at the **Royal Hua Hin Golf Course** and there are several restaurants serving delicious prawns and kingfish, squid and steamed crab.

Some 30km (18 miles) to the north of Hua Hin, the sister resort of **Cha-am** is famous for its beaches lined with casuarina trees and its seafood.

Further to the south are the impressive tear-shaped mountains of **Khao Sam Roi Yot National Park**★, which is well worth a visit. King Mongkut conducted an expedition here in August 1886 to witness the eclipse of the sun. Sadly, he died of malaria two months later.

Ko Phi Phi★★

Thailand's southern shores are dotted with small islands lapped by the waters of the Andaman Sea. Few are more idyllic than the two islands collectively known as Ko Phi Phi, although these days their charm is widely known.

Phi Phi Don is the largest of the two islands and can be reached by a two-hour boat ride from Phuket. You will arrive at the spectacular bay at **Ao Ton Sai**, where bungalows, overshadowed by steep limestone cliffs, now circle almost the entire island. **Hat Yao** has fine coral reefs and plenty of accommodation. If you want to get away from it all, rent a boat to take you around to **Hat Lanti** or further north to **Lo Bakao**.

One thing not to miss is the 30-minute scramble up to **Sunset Point** near the south-eastern tip of the island. From the viewpoint overlooking the crescent-shaped bays of Phi Phi Don, there is a magnificent **panorama★★★**.

Swimming, snorkelling and deep-sea fishing can be enjoyed from almost anywhere on the island. Glass-bottomed boats, canoe and motorboat tours and sailboat rentals are also available.

Phi Phi Le, the sister island, can be visited in an hour, but deserves the full day trip proposed by most operators. The first stop is the **Viking Cave★★★**, which contains prehistoric paintings as well as thousands of swallows' nests. The nests are believed to have aphrodisiac qualities and are sold in cities throughout Asia, where they are considered a delicacy.

After leaving the cave, you will be taken to **Maya Bay**, which boasts some of the most

The Viking Cave, on Phi Phi Le, is noted for its cave paintings and the thousands of swallows' nests which cluster on the sheer cliff face.

extraordinary scenery in the whole of southern Thailand. You can snorkel in the crystal-clear water before returning to Ao Ton Sai in the late afternoon.

Ko Samui★★★

This beautiful and increasingly popular island – now accessible by air from Bangkok – is rapidly following in Phuket's footsteps as an international jet-setters' paradise. Ko Samui is more relaxed though and less developed, with endless coconut plantations and tropical bungalows where you can sit out under the light of the moon.

The fashionable set tends to visit **Cha Weng Beach★★★**, a stunning crescent of

Cha Weng Beach, on Ko Samui, offers fine white sand and a range of watersports such as wind-surfing.

white sand to the east, or the more exclusive **Choeng Mon★**. Quieter souls may be more interested in **Lamai★★**, a bay which lies to the south, with bungalows clustered along a succession of small bays. Further to the west is **Big Buddha Beach**, offering fine views.

There are also plenty of watersport activities: you can sail, dive, wind-surf, deep-sea fish or, alternatively, go for a massage. Inland, there are several waterfalls, including **Hin Lat**, which cascades over several levels, and **Na Muang**, where three former kings have left their initials on the rocks.

Thirty kilometres (19 miles) to the north-west of Ko Samui is the spectacular **Mu Ko**

The series of smaller coves of Lamai Bay, on Ko Samui, are more secluded.

Ang Thong Marine National Park★★★. Many of the 30 islands have been named according to their strange shapes – **Sleeping Cow Island** and **Tripod Island** are just two examples. For a perfect day's outing visit the stunning beach on **Ko Mae** (Mother Island), but be sure to choose a day when the weather is clear and remember to bring suntan lotion and a hat.

If you are looking for a more extended getaway, continue further afield to **Ko Phangan**. This island covers 190 sq km (73 square miles) and has beaches and bungalows in abundance. The main places to stay are on **Hat Rin Beach**. Pretty bays can be found further round at **Hat Khuat** and **Chalok Lam**.

Picturesque **Ko Tao** lies even further afield, but this small island offers some of the best diving in the region. Coral coves are numerous, although you will find some white sandy beaches.

Krabi★★

Boats depart for **Ko Phi Phi★★** and several beaches in the vicinity from this little fishing village to the south of Phuket. **Ao Phra Nang★★** can be reached by a 15-minute boat ride and offers a spectacular little beach framed by limestone cliffs and the offshore island of **Ko Rang Nok**. Inside **Tham Phra Nang** (Princess Cave) you will find not only a hidden lagoon, but limestone phalluses offered by the local fishermen to ensure a plentiful catch.

Ao Nang, further up the coast, has a long curving beach with hotels and bungalows which can be reached by a road that winds through limestone cliffs.

One last attraction in the vicinity is the

Krabi has a busy fishing harbour, and is the docking point for the island ferries.

'Shell Cemetery' of **Su San Hoi**, situated 18km (12 miles) to the west of Krabi. The giant slabs of fossilised shells are believed to be 75 million years old, but remember that you will only be able to see them at low tide.

Boats from Krabi also leave for the impressive and still relatively undeveloped island of **Ko Lanta Yai**.

Nakhon Si Thammarat★★
This city, 780km (484 miles) south of Bangkok, is one of the oldest settlements in Thailand. It has several fine temples, including the 10C **Wat Phra Mahathat★★**, as well as the popular **National Museum★**. It is

also well known for its niello ware (a silver and black alloy used for jewellery and ornaments) and its shadow-puppets made from buffalo hide.

Phuket★★★

This island is the largest and best known in Thailand. Connected to the mainland by a small bridge, the 'Pearl of the South' encompasses more than 40km (25 miles) of white beaches, with countless resort areas and a dazzling selection of hotels.

Although Phuket (pronounced 'pooket') has had more than its fair share of development over the last decade, you can still find deserted stretches of sand and inland waterfalls and craggy rocks. There is a host of different activities to enjoy too, ranging from water-based sports such as

Karon Beach, on Phuket island, is less developed than Patong, with a long, curved beach.

A typically ornate gate decoration, Phuket.

snorkelling and sailing, to feasting on specialities of the region, including the most mouthwatering of all local delicacies, the Phuket lobster.

The beaches on the island all have their own different character. Partygoers prefer **Patong Beach★★★** where the night clubs keep on pounding until the early hours. Further south is **Karon Beach★★** with its long curving bay dotted with upmarket hotels. **Kata Beach★★**, situated beyond the magnificent headland, has several resorts and a sprinkling of bungalows. For something more exclusive, try **Surin** or **Pansea**, home to the legendary Amanpuri Hotel.

Situated on the tip of **Panwa Cape**, the **Phuket Aquarium & Marine Biological Research Centre★★** has over 100 varieties of fish, including the squirrel fish and the

amazing butterfly fish, which changes
colour.

On historic Ranong Road in **Phuket
Town★**, you can admire the Sino-Portuguese
architecture, a reminder of the days in the
late 19C when this was a prosperous tin-
mining centre inhabited by large numbers

The wild and rugged headland of Promthep is a well-known spot to watch the beautiful sunsets across the Andaman Sea.

of Chinese and Portuguese.

At **Mai Khao** and **Nai Yang** to the north, sea turtles occasionally come ashore at night between October and February to lay their eggs in the sand.

A short distance south of **Nai Harn Beach★★** is **Promthep Point**. This is the perfect place to round off the day and enjoy one of the many spectacular sunsets over the Andaman Sea.

Excursions from Phuket

The coastline around Phuket has more than its share of attractions. A hundred kilometres (62 miles) to the east of Phuket Town is **Phangnga Bay★★★**, made famous in the James Bond movie *The Man with a Golden Gun*. These staggering limestone cliffs reach up to 304m (1 000ft) in height and were formed about 10 000 years ago. Tours generally take in the Muslim fishing village of **Ko Panyi**, as well as **Ko Tapu** (Nail Island), which rises impossibly from the sea. Keep your eyes open, too, for the cliff paintings at **Khao Khian**, some of Thailand's earliest prehistoric remains.

Even more exciting, especially for younger visitors, are trips to the **hongs**, or inner caves. These tours, conducted in specially designed eco-sensitive dinghies, will take you into caves past giant stalactites and stalagmites illuminated only by the light of a torch. Inside, you will discover secret lagoons concealed by sheer walls of limestone.

For those in search of something a little different, a visit to the **Naga Noi Pearl Farm**, 22km (14 miles) north of Phuket Town, is an interesting experience. A few years ago, this cultured-pearl farm hit the record books when it produced the world's largest cultured pearl, measuring a massive 40mm (1½ inches) in diameter.

There are day cruises from Patong Beach to **Ko Phi Phi★★**, although these beautiful islands deserve a longer visit if possible. Tours can also be organised to the **Similan★★** and **Surin Islands** and the **Tarutao Islands★**, three of southern Thailand's most important marine national parks.

Surat Thani

Surat Thani, although primarily the departure point for passengers travelling to the islands of **Ko Samui★★★** and **Ko Phangan**, can also be used as a base to explore the historic town of **Chaiya★**.

This ancient settlement is believed to have been a regional capital of the Srivijaya Empire (13C). You can visit the 8C **Wat Phra Boromathat★★**, a survival from those times, or **Wat Kaeo**, which contains a dilapidated *stupa* (pagoda). Other artefacts have been moved to the **National Museum** in Bangkok (*see* p.29).

Tour boats regularly visit the famous 'James Bond' rock in Phangnga Bay.

WEATHER

Thailand's weather can be summed up in one word: tropical. For six months of the year it is generally dry and for the other six months of the year it is generally monsoonal, with cloudy skies and frequent downpours.

For the best weather, visit Thailand between November and February when the skies are clear and the temperatures pleasant. In Bangkok, temperatures average 87°F (31°C). In parts of the north and the north-east you may even need a sweater.

March to May is the hottest time of the year, with temperatures reaching as high as 103°F (40°C). From July to October, the weather is hot and wet. Rainfall averages 1 438mm (58 inches) and either comes in sudden downpours or drizzles for several hours on end.

In southern Thailand there is a greater variation in the climate throughout the year. Often when it is raining on one coast, it can be sunny on the other.

Dress comfortably – shorts and a T-shirt will be fine – but remember that in some hotels you may be required to wear more formal attire (jacket and tie).

CALENDAR OF EVENTS

Thailand's Buddhist religion and the people's love of fun ensure a full calendar of festivals and celebrations. Since many festivals have their dates set according to the phase of the moon, obtain a calendar from the tourist authorities on arrival. Here are some highlights.

The Elephant Festival, Bangkok, is a colourful and impressive spectacle.

February
Makha Bucha, Nationwide
One of Buddhism's most important religious festivals, this commemorates the preaching of the Buddha to 1 250 monks. Merit-making ceremonies and candle-lit processions are held in temples nationwide.
Flower Festival, Chiang Mai
Enjoy colourful floats, processions and the inevitable beauty contest in one of Thailand's most fun-loving towns.

March
Phra Phutthabat Fair, Saraburi
An annual pilgrimage to the revered Temple of the Holy Foot Print. You will be entertained by plays, musical events and much merit-making.

Mid April
Songkran, Nationwide
Although officially Thailand starts its New
Year on 1 January, Songkran is when the
locals celebrate the Thai New Year. Pageants
include traditional Buddhist ceremonies,
the sprinkling of water for good luck, and
major water battles. Prepare for a soaking!

May
Rocket Festival, Yasothon
Enjoy sheer mayhem as home-made rockets
with up to 110kg (242 pounds) of explosives
are fired into the clouds in the hope that
they will bring rain.
Royal Ploughing Ceremony, Bangkok
A traditional Brahmanic rice-planting
ceremony held annually in Sanam Luang,
over the road from the Grand Palace.
Visakha Bucha, Nationwide
This religious holiday recalls the date of the

The origins of the strange Masked Festival at Dansai remain a mystery.

Buddha's birth, enlightenment and death. Candle-lit processions are held inside temples throughout the country.

June
Masked Festival, Dansai
Nobody knows why this ancient festival started or what it signifies, but the two-day masked procession held in the tiny village of Dansai is undoubtedly one of Thailand's most unusual festivals. Locals don phalluses and parade through the streets.

The Candle Festival of Ubon Ratchathani provides an opportunity for women to parade in their bright costumes.

July
Candle Festival, Ubon Ratchathani
To celebrate the beginning of the rains, local people in Ubon and other towns in the north-east carry intricately carved giant candles to the local temples. The processions are accompanied by dances and beauty parades.

The boat race is taken very seriously, as the teams battle it out to win the competition.

September
International Swan-boat Races, Bangkok
Boat-racing teams from around the region compete in this highly prized competition held near Rama IX Bridge.

September/October
Vegetarian Festival, Phuket
The predominantly Chinese population of Phuket Island become vegetarian for a week. They also skewer themselves with spikes and walk on red-hot coals to make merit and to show the power of mind over matter.

November

Phimai Boat Races, Phimai Town

To celebrate the building of the magnificent temple of Phimai, there is a light and sound show as well as boat racing on the nearby Phimai river.

Loi Krathong, Nationwide

In this, Thailand's most beautiful festival, local people float small boats made out of banana leaves on the lakes and canals nationwide. The festival symbolises renewal. To enjoy Loi Krathong at its best, visit the town of Sukhothai.

Elephant Roundup, Surin

Elephant boxing matches, elephants playing football and elephants playing tug of war. These and other less bizarre activities are featured at the annual round up, renowned as the largest of its kind worldwide.

River Kwai Festival, Kanchanaburi

A fantastic light and sound show is held to recall the men who died building the historic bridge over the River Kwai.

Elephants await their turn to participate in the bizarre events at the Elephant Roundup, Surin.

December
King's Birthday, Nationwide

Thais celebrate the birthday of their much revered king, Rama IX, with processions and temple ceremonies.

ACCOMMODATION

There is a huge choice of accommodation in Thailand, ranging from luxury internationally renowned hotels, with every possible amenity, to beachside huts with little more than a thin mattress on the floor. Inbetween, there is a whole range of hotels, guesthouses, motels, hostels, houseboats, Chinese-style inns and bungalow complexes (popular with wealthy Thais) to suit every pocket. Listings of accommodation and rates are available from Tourism Authoriy of Thailand offices (see p.125).

Although staying at a top-class hotel in Thailand can cost as much as it does in the West, further down the scale comparable hotels of a good standard are cheaper. Guesthouses are cheaper still, many of which are adapted private homes and usually provide meals, but facilities will be basic and usually communal. It is as well to know that some cheap hotels can double as brothels.

A rough guide to prices (per room per night) is as follows:

Luxury: 3 000 up to 50 000 baht
Mid-range: 1 000 to 3 000 baht
Budget: 100 to 1 000 baht

Advance booking is recommended for more expensive accommodation during the high season (October-March). Out of season, independent travellers can obtain quite substantial discounts almost everywhere.

Recommendations

Bangkok

Oriental, 48 Oriental Avenue ☎ 02 236 0400. This well known luxury-priced hotel, frequented by the rich and famous, will be beyond the budgets of many travellers, but drop in for cocktails and a flavour of the beautifully preserved buildings.

Shrangri-La Hotel, 89 Soi Wat Suan Phlu, Charoen Krung Road ☎ 02 236 7777. Another hotel in the expensive price range, the Shrangri-La has spectacular views over the river.

The Sukhothai, 13/3 South Sathorn Road ☎ 02 287 0222 offers luxurious accommodation in stunning buildings (modern, but in classical Thai style), set in beautiful gardens with lotus ponds and courtyards. The Thai and Italian restaurants are excellent.

For mid-range hotels, the Sukhumwit Road area offers a wide choice and is well-situated for local shops and restaurants, but is rather distant from the main sights. The small but comfortable **Mermaid's Rest**, Soi 8, Sukhumwit Road ☎ 02 253 5123 has a swimming pool and pleasant garden. **The Landmark**, 138 Sukhumwit Road ☎ 02 245 0404 and the **Impala**, 9 Soi 24, Sukhumwit Road ☎ 02 259 2896 are both well located and offer good facilities.

Chiang Mai

Gap's House, 3 Soi 4, Ratchadamneon Road ☎ 053 278140 is value for money and has good facilities, with traditional buildings, antiques and a garden setting.

The Galare Guesthouse, 7/1 Charoen Prathet Road ☎ 053 249088 is well-situated, overlooking the river, and offers excellent value. For those with a more extensive budget, more luxurious hotels are centred around the night bazaar, such as the **Chiang Mai Plaza**, 92 Sri Dornchai Road ☎ 053 270036.

Phuket

At the top end of the price range is the legendary **Amanpuri Resort**, 118/1 Pansea Beach ☎ 076 311394, a complex of deluxe bungalows set in secluded grounds with a private beach.

A similar set-up, but more modestly-priced, is offered by **Jungle Beach Resort**, 11/3 Wiset Road Ao Sane Beach ☎ 076 381108.

FOOD AND DRINK

Some people come to Thailand just for the food. Whether you like fearsome curries or deliciously mild coconut soups, you will find something that fits the bill. Don't be put off by the label 'spicy' either. If you do not like chilli, simply order *mai phet* 'not hot'.

Lemongrass, galangal, tamarind, ginger and sweet basil are just some of the spices that go into making a Thai meal, as well as coriander, garlic and kaffir-lime leaves. To these ingredients are added *nam pla*, a pungent sauce made from fermented fish, some dried pink shrimps – and lashings of chillis.

Chicken, beef, pork and occasionally water buffalo can then be added to the wok, or, for those who prefer seafood, fresh fish, giant clams and succulent prawns. There is a mouthwatering choice of vegetables, too, from morning glory to aubergines,

Water melons for sale, Central Thailand.

tomatoes, Chinese cabbage and even French beans.

You may want to start off with something mild like a *tom ka kai*. This popular dish is made from spicy chicken cooked in coconut milk and is normally accompanied by plain rice, *khao phao*.

When you have got used to the food, try the famous *tom yam,* or lemongrass soup, a pungent broth that is made from lemongrass root, onions, tomatoes and, of course, chillis. Another dish which should not be missed is *yam nua ,* a spicy salad made with beef and chillis.

Simpler dishes without the spices include *khao phat,* fried rice, as well as fried noodles and mixed vegetables. If you don't know the Thai words – just point.

For those who prefer something a little more familiar, Bangkok and the major cities also offer fine European restaurants with the very best in French, German, Italian and even British cuisine. Most hotels and bungalows serve toast, coffee and sometimes even eggs and sausages for breakfast.

Local Delicacies

Although some dishes are available all over Thailand, there is plenty of regional diversity. Isan food, from the arid north-east region, is especially popular. Barbecued chicken, known as *kai yang*, is a favourite. Other dishes such as *larb moo* (minced pork) or *som tam*, a salad made from grated unripe papaya, garlic and chillis, tend to be considerably spicier. You will find that they are generally served with glutinous rice known as *khao nieo*.

In the north, nobody should miss a Kantoke dinner, a speciality which dates back to the times of the Lanna kingdom. Seated around a low, round table, you will be served a pork curry, fried pork skin and a chicken and vegetable curry and afterwards entertained with northern classical dances.

In the south, you can order fish-kidney curry, known as *kaeng tai pla*, although it may be so hot that you will literally burn. Otherwise try *tom ka kung*, a delicious mix of coconut milk and prawn or *pla priow wan*, a sweet and sour fish.

Finally, there is no shortage of mouthwatering desserts in Thailand. Often sweet and scented, they are almost invariably beautifully presented. For something special, try a coconut custard or an egg-yoke cake. Otherwise, take your pick from the delightful selection of fruits known as *pom la mai*. This will include anything from pineapples to lychees, tangerine oranges, papaya and mango.

Tips for Overseas Visitors

Although Thais are as easy-going with their food as they are in everyday matters, there are a few points of table etiquette worth remembering. When eating with Thai people, try not to finish all the food on your plate or in the serving dishes, as this suggests you have not been given a large enough portion.

Eat with a spoon and fork, which allows you to scoop up the rice. Noodles may be eaten with chopsticks. Most western restaurants will be able to offer you knives and forks.

When ordering from a menu, choose a selection of dishes and share. All the dishes are likely to arrive together and you can then help yourself to rice and take two or three small spoonfuls from each dish. Don't take vast quantities though. Thais eat slowly and leave themselves time and space to come back for more.

Beer and whisky are commonly drunk with meals. Ask for **Mekong** whisky or **Singha** beer for a taste of the local brew. Wine is available in most western restaurants, but is generally not served with Thai food. Bottled water can be purchased in many stores. Alternatively, ask for *nam phao* and you will be given a jug of boiled water. *Nam cha* (tea) is another popular drink, especially in Chinese restaurants.

Remember, too, that Thais generally eat early, with last orders at 9.30pm in most restaurants.

Finally, as the Thais say, *sanuk dee* – enjoy.

SHOPPING

In parts of Thailand you will find a variety of goods and prices that will appeal to all tastes and budgets. Things to buy range from traditional handicrafts to antiques, pottery and a vast display of wooden carvings.

Thailand excels in the production of leather and shoes, bags and jackets are available in almost all the major cities. In Bangkok, tailor-made suits, made-to-measure shirts and silk dresses are popular, although you should be extremely selective. Beautiful hand-woven silks in all weights and sizes make wonderful gifts.

Marvels are also created in silver. To see examples of design, you need only saunter past the shops in most tourist centres, especially Chiang Mai. Gems, including native sapphires, rubies or Burmese jade, offer bargains to seasoned collectors, but, more often than not turn out be coloured glass. Better to opt for lacquerware, a traditional art in which bamboo frames are sprayed repeatedly with a fine coat of black lacquer then painted over with bright colours.

Chiang Mai's famous umbrellas are also a popular item amongst tourists. Made from mulberry paper stretched over giant bamboo spokes, they are beautifully painted by hand.

You will see wooden carvings, too, along with thousands of purported 'antiques', as well as Buddha statues and armlets. Note, however, that any religious item will need a special export permit. Also, while there are plenty of genuine antiques, there are just as many fakes.

Specialist shops and department stores are

These beautifully made paper flowers make unusual souvenirs and gifts.

excellent in Thailand, but you can also find some of the best buys in the street markets.

Bangkok

Chatuchak For a bewildering choice of items ranging from snakes to exotic plants and elegant ceramic pots, try Thailand's famous weekend market near the southern end of Chatuchak Park. Here you will find things that you would never have dreamed existed. To avoid the crowds arrive early and remember, the market is only open on Saturdays and Sundays.

Open-air markets are found in every major town and city throughout Thailand, selling a variety of clothes and snacks.

Patpong Night Market is situated in Bangkok's well-known red-light district. It offers every sort of fake, from T-shirts to handbags, and much more.

Jim Thompson's on Surawong Road has a reputation as Thailand's top supplier of silk. Table mats, cushions and even wedding dresses can all be purchased, although for cheaper material you will need to look further afield.

Mahboonkrong This vast shopping complex near **Siam Square** packs in countless small shops and vendors, along with department stores and restaurants. It's cheap, cheerful and extremely crowded.

Chiang Mai

Night Market Chiang Mai's most popular market on Chang Khlan Road is a veritable hot-house of bargains, from silks to triangular cushions and stone reliefs.

Bo Sang This famous village, 9km (6 miles) outside Chiang Mai, is

renowned for its colourful umbrellas.
Nearby villages specialise in silver, porcelain
and lacquerware.

Khorat (Nakhon Ratchasima)

This town in the north-east is well known for
its silks. In some villages you can watch the
entire silk-making process, from the silk
worms feeding on mulberry leaves to the
final spinning of the yarn.

ENTERTAINMENT AND NIGHTLIFE

Bangkok

Entertainment is a big industry in Bangkok. Whether it is bars and nightclubs or boxing matches, cinemas or traditional classical dances you are after, you will always find something to please: the only thing the city doesn't provide is an excuse for an early night.

Almost everybody has heard of **Patpong**,

the raunchy strip of bars that has become Bangkok's best-known entertainment centre. Situated in the city centre off **Silom Road**, this comprises not only go-go bars, but a bewildering choice of 'shows', discotheques and gay bars, along with markets and restaurants.

Establishments generally open around 6.30pm, although most bars do not fill up until after 9pm when the shows start in the upstairs bars. Before entering any bar, always check the price of drinks and enquire to see if there is a cover charge. Fantastic bills are not unknown, especially in the upstairs bars.

Patpong, in Bangkok, is full of discos, clubs and go-go bars.

Fortunately there is more to this thriving metropolis than Patpong. At **Round Midnight Pub** on Soi Langsuan and **Brown Sugar** on Soi Sarasin you will find good jazz bars, while at **Saxaphone**, near Victory Monument, there is live music every night. There are plenty of trendy nightclubs as well, including **Phoebus**, the vast amphitheatre dancehall on Ratchadapisek Road which can handle capacity crowds of 9 000 and which is often full to the brim at weekends.

For something a little less hectic and more upmarket, try the **Bamboo Bar** in the exclusive Oriental Hotel. There are English films at **Siam Square** and at **Mahboonkrong**, with listings shown in the *Bangkok Post* and the *Nation* newspapers.

Elsewhere you will find classical dinner-dances held in many tourist restaurants, as well as the occasional performance of classical dance held in the **Thai Cultural Centre** or the **National Theater**.

Ask for the local giveaway magazine or visit the tourist information office to see what's on.

Girls in traditional costumes perform Lanna-style dancing in Chiang Mai.

Provincial Nightlife

Phuket, Pattaya and Chiang Mai may not be able to compete with Bangkok's nightlife, but there is nevertheless plenty going on. **Phuket** now has sunset cruises, classical dances, video bars, discos, nightclubs, girlie bars and gay bars. The biggest strip of bars is located in **Patong**. This is also the place for discotheques such as the **Banana Disco** and the **Crocodile Disco**.

Pattaya has an even more mind-boggling display of bars, many of which you would not want to take the family to. The town's biggest discotheque, the **Palladium**, ranks only narrowly behind Bangkok's Phoebus, with capacity crowds of 6 000. There are famous transvestite shows at **Alcazar** and **Tiffany's**.

Chiang Mai is more restrained. Nightlife there consists of smaller bars or Kantoke dinners accompanied by Lanna-style traditional dancing. Fine bands can be heard at the **Riverside** and at the **Brasserie** and most of the big hotels have their own discotheques.

Outside the major towns and cities, nightlife is often limited to restaurants, karaoke bars and the local village brothel.

SPORTS AND ACTIVITIES

Whether you are a spectator or a participant, Thailand offers plenty of international sports ranging from golf to paragliding, as well as its own national specialities, such as kite flying and Thai kick-boxing. There's no need to be an expert either. Instruction is available at all levels and you can hire almost everything from scuba gear to golf clubs and tennis rackets.

Modern Sports

Thailand has well over 100 **golf** courses
spread over the country, many of which have
been designed by some of the world's top
golfing names. These days it even hosts
international tournaments. Most courses are
open to non-members, but you should
always check on green fees and the cost of
caddies – and make an advanced booking if
you intend to play at weekends.

Swimming pools and **tennis** courts are
widely available in the big international
hotels, particularly those catering for
business people. You will also in many cases
find **beauty salons**, **jacuzzis**, **saunas** and
gymnasiums. Visitors who are not staying in
the hotel can sometimes pay a daily fee to
use the facilities.

Jogging is popular in the major cities and
at dawn and dusk Bangkok's **Lumphini Park**
is filled with runners as well as local people
practising **tai-chi**, **ball-room dancing** or
weight lifting.

Traditional Sports

Despite a passion for football and a growing
interest in other western sports, Thais
reserve their greatest enthusiasm for
traditional sports.

'**Muay thai**' or Thai kick-boxing, is viewed
more as an art than as a normal sport.
Boxers not only use their hands, but also
their feet and their knees and elbows.
Popular places to witness the spectacle
include Bangkok's **Lumphini Stadium** on
Rama IV Road and **Ratchadamnoen Stadium**
on Ratchadamnoen Nok Avenue. For the
best views, get ringside seats. For colour and
frantic local betting, join the third-class
ticket holders at the back.

Kite flying is especially popular during the months from February to April when contests are held in Bangkok's **Sanam Luang**. Other sports you may come across include *takraw*, in which players knock around a rattan ball with elbows, heads or feet, as well as **long-boat racing** and illegal **fish fighting**.

Beach and Watersports

Given Thailand's steamy climate and magnificent coastline, it is not surprising that watersports are immensely popular. Take your pick from the range of activities available, from paragliding, scuba-diving and deep-sea fishing to more daring persuits such as bunjie jumping. You can also waterski and jet ski, while the more sedate may prefer to paddle a kayak. In the major southern resorts, you can even rent a boat and set sail to discover your own little island.

Phuket and **Ko Samui** are the best centres for most watersports, with shops catering for every need and standard. **Pattaya** also offers diving courses from beginner to advanced level.

Other destinations offer different rewards. The **Similan Islands**, the **Surin Islands** and **Tarutao Island National Park** have magnificent corals and rich marine life. The small island of **Ko Tao**, reached from Ko Samui, also has some of the finest diving waters in Thailand. For amateurs with their flippers and face mask, **Ko Phi Phi** and **Krabi** are very rewarding.

The best time of year for sailing or diving is between November and April. From May to October, you may encounter monsoon rains and gusting winds.

THE BASICS

Before You Go

All visitors entering Thailand must possess a valid passport. Nationals of most countries, including the UK, European countries, Canada, Australia, New Zealand and the US, can stay in Thailand for up to 30 days providing they possess a confirmed outward ticket. For longer stays, visas can be obtained (tourist visa, 60 days; non-immigrant visa, 90 days) from all Thai embassies and consulates abroad or at Bangkok, Chiang Mai, Phuket and Hat Yai international airports on arrival. Anyone staying beyond the limits stipulated on their visa will be fined 100 *baht* per day.

No vaccinations are necessary for entry into Thailand, but travellers from areas where cholera or yellow fever are present may be required to produce the relevant vaccination certificates.

It is recommended that polio, tetanus, typhoid and hepatitis-A inoculations be kept up to date, especially for those travelling independently in rural areas. It is also sensible to take malaria tablets; consult your doctor for advice in good time before leaving home.

Getting There

Most visitors to Thailand arrive at Bangkok's Don Muang International Airport, 22km (14 miles) from the city. There are daily flights from Europe, North America, Asia and Australasia. Other international flights, mostly from Singapore, Kuala Lumpur, Penang and Hong Kong, land at the southern airports of Phuket and Hat Yai, and at Chiang Mai in northern Thailand. Flights should be booked well in advance, particularly over the Christmas period. An airport tax is charged on departure (250 *baht*).

The options by rail are from Singapore, Kuala Lumpur and Butterworth in Malaysia. In Bangkok, all trains arrive and depart from Hualamphong Station, Rama IV Road.

By road, it is only possible to enter Thailand via Malaysia. There are three border crossings which close late afternoon. Remember that Malaysia is one hour ahead of Thai time, so when travelling from Thailand the border crossing closes an hour earlier than from the Malaysian side.

Arriving

From the airport at Bangkok there are various ways of getting to the city, including a regular coach and private limousine service, airport buses, shuttle buses, public buses (crowded and uncomfortable, but very cheap) and taxis. Only registered airport taxis, bearing a yellow licence plate, should be taken. They are available at authorised Public Taxi Stands, where the fares to various destinations are posted; beware of other drivers offering their services at cheaper rates.

Whichever way you go, the journey can take up to an hour and a half.

The main train station is in central Bangkok in Rama IV Road. (*See* **Getting There**)

Car hire firms have offices at Don Muang International Airport but unless you intend to do a lot of touring, driving is neither the most relaxing or cost-effective way of travelling around Thailand; driving yourself around Bangkok should not even be contemplated.

There are no regular ferry services to Thailand.

A series of seated Buddhas at Wat Ratchaburana, Ayutthaya.

Accidents and Breakdowns

Car accidents are fairly commonplace in Thailand and adequate insurance is essential. In the event of an accident or breakdown, contact the tourist police (*see* **Police**). If you are in a hire car, you should be able to call upon the rental firm for help so carry their details with you at all times. Avoid driving in Bangkok.

Accommodation see p.96

Airports see Getting There

Babysitters see Children

Banks

Banks are open from 8.30am-3.30pm, Monday to Friday. Money can either be changed here or in the numerous exchange offices to be found in all tourist areas, which are open much longer hours. Travellers' cheques can be exchanged at the larger branches; take your passport with you.

Beaches

With over 2 500km (1 562 miles) of coastline and plenty of sunshine, the beaches of Thailand are among its major attractions. The choice ranges from deserted, palm-fringed beaches and the quiet coves of unspoilt islands, to busy seaside resorts with superb stretches of sand where entertainment can be found round the clock.

Opportunities for deep-sea game fishing, scuba diving and snorkelling are among the best south-east Asia has to offer, and other watersports such as wind surfing, water-skiing and sailing are readily available. As far as children are concerned, the beaches are clean and most are safe (though beware of rip tides and strong currents on some islands), and many resorts offer beach activities for them, too. Beware of getting sunburnt. Sunbathing in the nude is illegal in Thailand.

Bicycles

These are readily available for

hire in all tourist areas and are a good way of getting around, with the exception of Bangkok, where the traffic is a nightmare. Most towns have small bicycle-hire shops or stands and many hotels and guesthouses have bicycles that can be hired for the day or week. Check that the bike is in good working order before setting off.

Books
Here are a few reading suggestions to enhance your stay in Thailand.
Thailand – The Lotus Kingdom, by Alistair Shearer
Borderliner, by Charles Nicholl
Isaan: Forgotten Provinces of Thailand, by Ben Davies

Breakdowns see **Accidents**

Buses see **Transport**

Camping
In general, camping in Thailand is restricted to the national parks, where tents can also be rented, and a few of the islands. Pitching a tent outside these areas is not recommended. For further information, contact the National Park Division, Royal Forestry Department, Phahonyothin Road, Bangkok ☎ 02 579 5262/579 0529.

Brightly coloured umbrellas adorn the white sands of Phuket beach.

Car Hire

Hiring a car from one of the international firms is the best bet, or from a company recognised by the Tourism Authority of Thailand. Jeeps are very popular. The minimum age for hiring a car is 21 (although there can be supplements for under 25s) and a valid international driving licence must be held. Make sure you have adequate insurance (it is not automatically included by all local companies) and check the spare tyre and brakes before setting off. Most large firms can arrange the hire of chauffeur-driven vehicles, as can bigger hotels. If you are staying in Bangkok, don't even attempt to drive yourself around. See **Driving**

Children

Children are warmly received in Thailand and you will quickly be made to feel at home if you have any with you. The fierce sun is a potential danger and the food may not be to every Western child's taste, but the bigger hotels will cater for their needs if asked. Babysitting arrangements vary, but it is always worth enquiring. Western brands of baby food and powdered milk may not be available every-where, although their equivalents will. Children under ten can travel free on trains and buses, but are not guaranteed a seat.

Churches see **Religion**

Climate see **p.90**

Clothing

Thin, light cotton or linen is the best type of clothing to wear. During the cool season (November to February) a sweater or jacket may be necessary, or if visiting the mountainous regions. Remember that no shorts, no bare shoulders or legs are permissible when visiting temples. Some restaurants and night-clubs require that men wear a jacket and tie.

Complaints

If any dispute cannot be satisfactorily resolved with the person in charge there and then, contact the Tourist Assistance Centre (TAC, ☎ 02 281 5051/282 8129), a special department of TAT. In emergencies, contact the English-speaking tourist police which have offices in all the main tourist areas.

Consulates

Embassies and consulates can be found in Bangkok:

Australia 37 Sathorn Road
☎ 02 287 2680
Canada Boonmitr Building,
11th and 12th Floor, 138 Silom
Road ☎ 02 234 1561/8
Eire United Flour Mills
Building, 11th Floor, 205
Ratchawongse Road
☎ 02 223 0876
New Zealand 93 Witthayu
Road ☎ 02 251 8165
UK 1031 Ploenchit Road
☎ 02 253 0191/9
US 95 Witthayu Road
☎ 02 252 5040/9

Crime

Violent crime is not common
in Thailand but it is wise to
take the usual precautions
against petty theft.

*Temple at Wat Phra That Doi
Suthep, Northern Region.*

• Carry as little money, and as
few credit cards, as possible,
and leave any valuables in the
hotel safe.
• Carry wallets and purses in
secure pocket, wear body belts,
or carry handbags across your
body or firmly under your arm.
• Cars can be a target for
opportunists, so never leave
your car unlocked, and hide
away or, better still, remove
items of value.
• To guard against being an
unwitting carrier of drugs,
always keep a close eye on your
luggage at airports, and never
carry parcels on behalf of
anyone else.
• Beware of buying gemstones
in Thailand unless you are
experienced. Many sold as
genuine are in fact fakes.

Currency see Money

Customs and Entry Regulations

It is strictly forbidden to take
any narcotics (hemp, opium,
cocaine, morphine and
heroin), obscene literature,
pictures or articles, or firearms
into Thailand. Certain fruits,
vegetables and plants are also
prohibited and permission
must be obtained to take an
animal into the country.

Personal effects and profes-
sional instruments can be

taken in free of duty, as can a litre of wine or spirits and up to 200 cigarettes.

Buddha images or antiques cannot be taken out of the country without a licence from the Department of Fine Arts; this can usually be arranged through the shop where you make your purchase.

Disabled Visitors

There are very few special facilities for disabled people in Thailand. The larger hotels, however, are becoming more conscious of this shortfall and any of the TAT offices (*see* **Tourist Information**) should be able to provide relevant advice and information.

Long-haul Holidays and Travel is available from RADAR, 12 City Forum, 250 City Road, London EC1V 8AF, ☎ 0171 250 3222 between 10am and 4pm. It contains advice and information about accommodation, transport, services, equipment and tour operators in many countries, including Thailand.

Driving

Cars drive on the left-hand side in Thailand and visitors must hold an international driving licence. Driving regulations are not always heeded so motoring can be something of a

hazardous business. Comprehensive insurance is essential.

One of the main points to be aware of is that the size of a vehicle determines priority, irrespective of who is on the major road. Speed limits are 40kph (25mph) in built-up areas, 80kph (50mph) on motorways. If these limits are exceeded the police can and do impose on-the-spot fines. Honking the horn indicates overtaking.

You should not attempt to drive in Bangkok, and driving after dark is best avoided.

Petrol is readily available at prices comparable to those in Europe.

Dry Cleaning *see* Laundry

Electric Current

The electric current throughout the country is 220V. Travellers are advised to carry a plug adaptor kit as a variety of plugs and sockets is in use.

Embassies *see* Consulates

Emergencies

Mobile police: ☎ 191
Tourist police: ☎ 1699
Tourist assistance: ☎ 02 282 5081/282 8129

Etiquette

Thai people are a conservative

and polite nation and due respect should be paid to their customs and religious beliefs. These include the following:

• Women should not be touched without their consent and demonstrative behaviour between a man and a woman is frowned upon.

• Pointing your foot at a person or object is considered rude.

• Swimming or sun-bathing in the nude is prohibited.

• When entering a temple, wear modest clothing and take your shoes off before entering the hall of worship.

• Images of the Buddha are sacred and sacrilegious acts regarding them can result in imprisonment.

• On no account must a woman touch a monk, give things to him directly or accept things directly from him.

• Do not criticise the monarchy or talk about the royal family with disrespect.

Excursions

Any of the larger hotels will be able to advise on local tours and day trips, as can travel centres.

The State Railway of

The Doi Inthanon National Park is an area of dramatic waterfalls.

Thailand organises economy tours to a number of destinations on weekends and national holidays.

Guidebooks

The *Michelin Green Guide Thailand* provides full information on the sights and attractions in Thailand, together with useful background information on the country.

Health

It is essential to take out comprehensive health insurance before leaving home because any medical or dental treatment has to be paid for on the spot. Check with your insurance company what documentation you need to obtain from a doctor, dentist or hospital in order to make a claim. Main hospitals have a 24-hour emergency unit where immediate treatment can be obtained.

The main risks to health are the heat and contamination from tap water and unpeeled fruit. To guard against these, wear a hat, use liberal high-factor sun-tan cream, drink plenty of fluids and be careful about what and where you eat. Children especially should be protected from these potential dangers.

Malaria can be a problem in the forested areas and some islands, but not in the cities or central plains. Nonetheless, it is a good idea to take a course of malaria tablets and to take precautions against being bitten by mosquitoes as much as possible.

A first-aid kit is a good idea and should include sterilized needles, insect repellent, insect-bite ointment, tablets for stomach upsets and plasters.

Be aware that sexually transmitted diseases and AIDS are prevalent. *See also* **Before You Go, p.112**

Hours *see* Opening Hours

Information *see* Tourist Information Offices

Language

Although English is widely understood in cities and tourist areas, and spoken (along with other European languages) in most hotels, shops and restaurants in the major tourist centres, an attempt at a few basic Thai words will be appreciated. Thai/English road names and signs are common.

Thai is a very complicated language and as there is no standard system of transliteration of Thai script into Roman, spellings of words, names and

> Hello / Sawatdee kap *(male)* ka *(female)*
>
> Goodbye / Sawatdee kap *(male)* ka *(female)*
>
> Yes / Kap *(male)* Ka *(female)*
>
> No / Mai
>
> Thank you / Kop khoon kap *(male)* ka *(female)*
>
> How much? / Taorai?
>
> Where is the … ? / … yu tinnay?
>
> I don't understand / Mai kao chai
>
> Excuse me / Kor thot

places differ widely wherever you see them. The use of five tones, each giving a different meaning to a single syllable, is an additional difficulty for Westerners trying to understand or speak the language.

Laundry

Coin-operated self-service establishments are very few and far between but this poses no problems as most hotels and guesthouses offer an excellent and cheap same-day laundry service.

Lost Property

If you lose something on public transport (bus or train), contact the local station. Otherwise contact the nearest tourist police station, where English is usually spoken ☎ 1699.

Medical Care see **Health**

Money

The unit of currency throughout Thailand is the Thai *baht* (Bt). It is divided into 100 *satang* (s). Banknotes come in denominations of 10, 20, 50, 500 and 1 000 *baht*, and coins in denominations of 25 and 50 *satang* and 1, 2, 5 and 10 *baht*.

There is no limit to the amount of Thai currency or any other type of foreign exchange that visitors may take into Thailand. All foreign exchange that has been brought in may freely be taken out again, but the maximum amount of Thai currency that can be taken out of the country without prior authorisation is 50 000 *baht* per person. Travellers visiting one of Thailand's neighbouring countries, however, may take up to 50 000 *baht* per person.

Money and travellers' cheques can either be changed at larger banks or exchange offices, which can be found everywhere in tourist areas and are open from about 8am-9pm or later, seven days a week. There is a 24-hour exchange office at Bangkok Airport.

Major international credit cards are accepted at most hotels, restaurants and shops in tourist areas, but may not be in more remote areas.

Newspapers

There are four English-language newspapers in Thailand – the *Bangkok Post*, the *Nation*, the *Thailand Times* and *Business Day* – which give local and international news and events. Major English-language newspapers and magazines are also widely available from supermarkets, bookshops, hotels, newsagents and department stores.

Opening Hours

Shopping malls are generally

A Lisu woman from the Chiang Rai Province drying chillies.

open from 10am-10pm, seven days a week. *See also* **Banks** and **Post Offices**

Photography

The major brands of film are widely available in Thailand and shops offering a 24-hour or less processing service are plentiful. The light is extremely bright, and cameras and film should be kept out of the intense heat. Some museums have restrictions on what exhibits can be pho-tographed, and photography is forbidden inside parts of the Grand Palace in Bangkok, but otherwise there are few restric-tions.

Police

In the event of any trouble or emergency contact the tourist police, set up in association with the Tourism Authority of Thailand to provide help and safety to tourists. Tourist policemen are stationed in major tourist areas and can be identified by their badge. Most speak English. In case of an emergency, contact the Tourist Police Centre, Unicohouse Building, Soi Lang Suan, Ploenchit Road, Bangkok ☎ 02 652 1721/6.

Post Offices

Post offices are open from 8am-8pm, Monday to Friday, and until 1pm on Saturdays. Stamps can be purchased there or in the larger hotels.

Public Holidays

Several of Thailand's festivals, which merit national holidays, are determined by the lunar calendar and therefore do not have fixed dates.

New Year's Day: 1 January
Makha Bucha (Full Moon
  Day): mid to late February
Chakri Day: 6 April
Songkran (Traditional Thai
  New Year): mid April
Labour Day: 1 May
Coronation Day: 5 May
Viskha Bucha (Full Moon
  Day): May
HM the Queen's Birthday:
  12 August
Chulalongkorn Day:
  23 October
HM the King's Birthday:
  5 December
Constitution Day:
  10 December
New Year's Eve: 31 December

Public Transport
see **Transport**

Religion

Thailand is predominantly a Buddhist country – with over 90 per cent of the population adhering to Theravada

Buddhism – but Christian churches are to be found in Bangkok and many of the provincial capitals. Services are held mainly in Thai, with some occasionally in English, French or German. Remember that any image of the Buddha is held to be sacred and must be treated with respect.

Smoking

In general the habit is widely tolerated, although it is banned in temples and should be avoided anywhere where there are connections with the royal family. There are signs saying No Smoking in buses, but you will find they are often ignored. Some taxis specify no smoking. Cigarettes can be bought practically everywhere.

Stamps see Post Offices

Taxis see Transport

Telephones

International calls can be made from booths in main post offices or from private international call offices. Phoning from your hotel is the most convenient method, but it will cost considerably more. Local directory assistance: ☎ 13
Domestic long distance: ☎ 101
International operator: ☎ 100

International assistance: ☎ 181
   Country codes are as follows:
Australia: 61
Canada: 1
Ireland: 353
New Zealand: 64
UK: 44
USA: 1
   Domestic calls can be made from any phone box: local calls can be made from red boxes, long-distance calls within Thailand from blue boxes; phonecards can be used in green boxes for both.

Time Difference

The time in Thailand is GMT minus seven hours. If you are crossing into Malaysia, note that the time is one hour ahead of Thai time.

Tipping

In the bigger and more expensive restaurants and hotels 10 per cent is normal if service has not been included, but elsewhere between 5 and 10 per cent is adequate. Taxi drivers do not expect a tip.

Toilets

Hotels in tourist areas have western-style toilets but elsewhere they are of the hole-in-the-ground variety. Public toilets are rare, but restaurants or shops do not mind if you use their facilities. Ask for

Hong nam. Toilet paper (not always provided) should be put in the bin provided.

Tourist Information Offices

Useful tourist information covering accommodation, tours, shopping, eating out, etc., is available from TAT (Tourism Authority of Thailand) offices throughout the country – open seven days a week from 8.30am-4.30pm – and in certain countries abroad.

The head office in Thailand is: 372 Ratchadamnoen Nok Road, Bangkok 10100 ☎ 02 226 0060.

Offices abroad include the following:

Australia (including New Zealand) Level 2, National Australia Bank House, 255 George Street, Sydney 2000 ☎ 247 7549/7540

Canada *see* US/Chicago
New Zealand *see* Australia
UK 49 Albermarle Street, London W1X 3FE
☎ 0839 300 800
US (including Canada)
The Americas Regional Office, 303 East Wacker Drive, Suite 400, Chicago, IL 60601
☎ 819 3990/5;
3440 Wilshire Boulevard, Suite 1100, Los Angeles CA 90010
☎ 382 2353/5;
5 World Trade Centre, Suite 3443, NY 10048
☎ 432 0433/0435

Tours *see* Excursions

Transport

Domestic flights are operated by Thai Airways International and Bangkok Airways. Between them they link Bangkok and practically all the other main towns in Thailand. Reserva-

Tuk-tuk driver with his vehicles.

tions should be made as flights book up quickly, particularly from Bangkok.

The railways in Thailand are run by the State Railway of Thailand and provide a comfortable, reasonably priced means of travelling about the country. Local trains usually have three classes, although slower trains may only have third class. Sleepers can be booked on longer trips. A train service operates between the city centre and Don Muang Airport, although it is not convenient. You can also travel by train into Malaysia and Singapore. Timetables are available from Bangkok Railway Station in Rama IV Road ☎ 02 223 7010/7020.
See also **Excursions**

A modern road system stretches to most parts of the country and the public bus service offers a fast, cheap means of getting around. Seating tends to be cramped, however, and a more comfortable, albeit slightly more expensive, option is the air-conditioned coach service. Both types of bus also operate in Bangkok and main towns.

Local public transport consists of taxis and samlors, known as *tuk-tuks* (three-wheeled taxi scooters). Always agree a price beforehand when taking the latter, which are really only suitable for short hops. Most taxis are fitted with a meter and hotel taxis have fixed tariffs.

River taxis along the Chao Phraya River are popular with tourists and are a good way of avoiding Bangkok's traffic. The Chao Phraya Express boats travel up and down stream with fares ranging from 5 to 15 *baht* per person. Private boats can be hired for about 400 *baht* an hour.

TV and Radio

Most big hotels in Thailand have satellite television and channels offering feature films and news programmes. There are also English-language radio stations on FM 95.5Mhz, 105Mhz and 107Mhz.

Vaccinations
see **Before You Go, p.112**

Water

You should drink only bottled or boiled water, both of which are widely available, as are ice cubes made from purified water.

INDEX

INDEX

THAILAND

— in your pocket —

11/24

MICHELIN®

Main Contributor: Ben Davis

Photograph Credits
All photos supplied by The Travel Library:
A Amsel back cover, title page, 25 (top), 32, 43, 84, 91,
115; A Birkett 31, 85; Ian Cruickshank 5, 37, 94, 103,
106; Ben Davis 6, 9, 11, 12, 13, 16, 17, 19, 20, 21, 23, 25
(bottom), 29, 35, 36, 38, 39, 41, 44, 45, 47, 49, 50, 51, 53,
60, 61, 65, 67 (right, left), 68, 69, 71, 73, 74, 75, 76, 78,
80, 81, 83, 86, 89, 92, 93, 95, 99, 105, 117, 119, 125; John
R Jones 34, 66, 108, 122; David Rose 63; Gino Russo
front cover, 30, 46, 48, 52, 54, 55, 57, 59, 113;
Ivor Wellbelove 62.

Front cover: Wat Phra Si Mahathat, Sukhothai; back cover:
Patong beach, Phuket; title page: umbrella painting, Borsang
village

While every effort is made to ensure that the information in this guide is as accurate and up-to-date
as possible, detailed information is constantly changing. The publisher cannot accept responsibility for
any consequences resulting from changes in information, errors or omissions.

MANUFACTURE FRANÇAISE DES PNEUMATIQUES MICHELIN
Société en commandite par actions au capital de 2 000 000 000 de francs
Place des Carmes-Déchaux – 63 Clermont-Ferrand (France)
R.C.S. Clermont-Fd 855 200 507
© Michelin et Cie. Propriétaires-Éditeurs 1997
Dêpôt légal Mai 97 – ISBN 2-06-651301-6 – ISSN en cours

Printed in Spain 4-97